How to gain
FINANCIAL
INDEPENDENCE

by Edward T. O'Toole

A Benjamin Company/Rutledge Book

SBN 671-10344-X

Library of Congress Catalog Card Number 69-10328
Copyright © 1969 by
Rutledge Books, Inc. and The Benjamin Company, Inc.
Published by
Rutledge Books, Inc.
and by
The Benjamin Company, Inc.
485 Madison Avenue
New York, New York 10022

Contents

The subject matter of this book is, by definition, dynamic, changing—sometimes from month to month—along with the economy of the United States. Nevertheless, the author assumes full responsibility for the facts he has presented—except for those, such as new laws and regulations, which cannot be foreseen at this stage.

Foreword

This book is essentially a book about consumer finance, and it is written for you, the average American consumer.

Books on consumer finance are not rare. There is no shortage of helpful manuals telling you how to earn more money, how to stretch your dollars, how to spend wisely and well, how to save, how to invest. While some of these books are better than others, almost all are helpful.

Why, then, another book on consumer finance? What new useful purpose can this one serve?

This book is distinguished from others because of its focal point. Unlike most of its predecessors, it does not focus on John Doe or Jane Doe as *individual* consumers. Rather it focuses on the *family*, on the theory that the average American earns, spends, saves and invests as part of a family unit.

The point of view of this book also is distinctly different. It reflects the conviction that although the average American family today enjoys comforts and luxuries unprecedented in mankind's history, at the same time millions of families suffer from a problem—a gnawing, chronic problem: paradoxically, the more affluent they become, the less control they have over their financial affairs. As their income rises, so do their debts—and unfortunately, in many instances, family tensions as well. Marriage counselors generally agree that financial difficulties are a common cause of divorce.

No magic—but sensible solutions

The fundamental problem confronting the family is implied in the title of this book: "How to Gain Financial Independence." Financial independence is not synonymous with riches. There are many rich American families, but this book is not for them.

But although they may never become rich, there are millions of families who can become financially independent, and it is to them that this book is addressed. Financial independence is determined not so much by the amount of money you have as by what you do with it. For money is quicksilver, as difficult to retain as it is to grasp. Yet the billions of dollars of personal savings in mutual savings banks testify that saving is a habit—not just a vast accumulation of money.

Don't expect this book to offer any magic solution to the problem of gaining and retaining financial independence. In these pages you will not meet Aladdin and his lamp, nor will Santa Claus put in an appearance. Instead, your first encounter will be with an American family, and you will soon see that it is in deep trouble.

Our family will not be a statistical replica of the average family. The head of the house makes more money, for one thing; but he spends more, too. There is no family that exactly matches the statistical average—no family, for example, with 2.7 children. However, the problems besetting our family, although they may differ in detail from your own and the one next door, are common ones.

The purpose of this book is to explore them and to offer sensible solutions.

Service centers for family financial needs

Where can people go for this kind of service and assistance? There are a number of places, but certainly among the most prominent are mutual savings banks.

These people-oriented banks operate in one-third of the states and in Puerto Rico, where they serve the savings, home financing and other financial needs of many millions of American families through some 1400 main offices and branches.

Savings banks are "mutual"—that is, they do not have stockholders and are operated in the mutual interests of their depositors. Savings banks are not the same as commercial banks, which are owned by stockholders who receive as dividends a major share of the bank earnings whether they are depositors or not. Mutual savings banks distribute all earnings to depositors after paying operating expenses and setting aside certain sums of money for essential reserves as required by law. They operate under government supervision and carry insurance of accounts.

Mutual savings banks have always specialized in serving the financial needs of individuals and families rather than commerce and industry. Over the past century and a half, the savings banks—above all other financial institutions—have been dedicated to serving families of moderate means and thus have gained recognition as "family financial service centers."

No place to save

Before the first savings banks were formed in Philadelphia and Boston in 1816, the average family had no financial institution it could call its own. The principal function of existing commercial banks was then, as it is now, to handle the funds and credit needs of business, industry and commerce. Commercials in the early 19th century did not accept small deposits from individuals.

Not that your average family a century and a half ago was heavily burdened with spare cash, for life in those days was a far cry from the affluent society of today. In 1816 the entire population of the United States was less than the current population of New York City. The nation consisted of only 17 states, all east of the Mississippi, and little else. Thirteen years earlier, the Louisiana Purchase had transferred title of a huge tract beyond the Mississippi from France to the United States, but this was still largely virgin territory. Florida would not be purchased from Spain until 1819; Texas would remain a separate, independent republic until 1845; California would not be ceded by Mexico until 1848.

The seeds of the industrial revolution in Britain had been carried across the Atlantic with the colonial settlers to the new nation's northeastern cities. By 1816, thousands of American families were earning their livelihood working in the factories and mills of America's mercantile ports. A new middle class was beginning to emerge.

Thrifty wage earners were discovering that by carefully watching their purchases they could save small sums of money. But where to put them? Remember, the commercial banks simply were not interested in the few dollars worth of savings accumulated by the workingman.

The concept of a mutual savings bank originated in Europe in the mind of a resourceful Scot, the Reverend Henry Duncan, minister for a poor parish in Ruthwell, Scotland. He saw the need for a local bank that would accept small savings, invest them and divide the earnings equally among the depositors, who in effect would be the bank's mutual owners. The idea quickly caught on and soon many savings banks were operating in the British Isles.

The success of these new institutions, dedicated as they were to giving the workingman and his family a secure place for husbanding the family's resources, led to the founding of the first mutual savings banks in the new world in the winter of 1816 in Philadelphia and Boston.

Enter the savings banks

The move could not have come at a more opportune time, for in 1820 the first wave of a gigantic tide of immigration rolled in from Europe, inundating the east coast and pushing into the Midwest. During the next century, more than 38 million new Americans were to arrive from Europe, and they found the savings banks ready, willing and able to serve their family financial needs.

As young America grew, savings banking grew, too. Around the time of the Civil War there were nearly 300 mutuals in New England and the Middle Atlantic states; after the Civil War, more were soon organized in Indiana, Wisconsin and Minnesota. In 1917 savings banks were established in the state of Washington; in 1931, in Oregon; and in 1961, Alaska joined what is today the $72 billion-plus mutual savings bank system. In 1966, the Commonwealth of Puerto Rico saw the introduction of savings banking within its borders.

Today the mutuals continue to be leaders in providing specialized financial services to American families. These include a wide variety of savings accounts tailored to the personal needs of savers, including special purpose and school savings. In addition, loans are made for home buying, home improvement, educational and personal needs. These may be passbook loans or, in 11 states, consumer loans. Savings bank life insurance is available in some states, among many other important services.

Family needs come first

While savings banks are chartered exclusively by the state in which they are based—unlike other financial institutions, they do not have the option of operating under a federal charter—their services in large part are national in scope. For example, depositors living in all 50 states and even in many foreign lands have their savings in more than 23 million savings bank accounts. They are also nationwide in their home financing. Currently some 5 million families in the 50 states and Puerto Rico are living in better housing being financed with the help of a savings bank mortgage.

9

As Senator J. William Fulbright of Arkansas has said, "Not only have mutual savings banks filled an investment gap for persons of limited means and provided a place for the safekeeping of small accounts, but they also have channeled additional savings into constructive investment. By proving that such an enterprise could succeed, they have stimulated the development of similar institutions and have led commercial banks to establish savings departments and to look more benevolently on small accounts and small borrowers."

Adolf A. Berle, Professor Emeritus of Columbia University Law School and a distinguished public servant and diplomat, has described the mutual savings bank as the average family's "financial adviser and trust company."

Professor Berle said, "Mutual savings banks are the managers for tens of billions of dollars of property, held in small quantities by millions of little people who cannot get the attention of high-powered commercial and investment communities. At a savings bank, the average American who is not wealthy should be able to find a complete program and package. It could include all or any of the following: Straight savings account; life insurance; moderate participation in equity; assurance of educational credit—all in responsible hands, and at a cost lower than like service is presently available to him, when it is available at all. The combination of savings and insurance on the intake side; of home mortgages and educational loans, preferably in cooperation with the educational institutions, on the credit side; and, when appropriate, mutual fund service to offer equity investment, make up the picture."

One result of such recognition of savings banking's history and its dedicated service to individual and family financial needs has been a strong movement toward the establishment of savings banks in all 50 states through enactment of federal legislation.

Chapter One

Money Mismanagement

At first glance you might say on meeting a couple we'll call the Atkinsons, "Everyone should have it so good."

Jeff and Phoebe Atkinson live in a city in upstate New York. They are in their late twenties and have two small children—Martha, age 7, and Martin, age 6. They rent a comfortable garden apartment in a suburban neighborhood only a half hour from Jeff's office downtown. Since graduating from a small but well-regarded college, Jeff has been working for a drug manufacturer. His present job as sales manager pays $12,800.

The Atkinsons—a rather typical suburban family—drive a station wagon. Phoebe uses it almost every day to take the children to school. Jeff uses it almost every weekend during the golfing season, and in the winter they all use it occasionally to drive up to Vermont for fun in the snow.

Indeed, at first glance you might find the Atkinsons a family to be envied.

But hold on there. Take a look behind the scenes. Why does Jeff delay to the last minute in opening his monthly bank statement? Why that worried frown when Phoebe sits down to make out her shopping list? Why have they been sniping at each other so much lately?

"You and that golf club! That's our problem," Phoebe says.

"No, it's you and your clothes—that's our problem," says Jeff.

The trouble with the Atkinsons

The fact is the Atkinsons are in deep trouble. And if they don't do something about it soon, their marriage could get into deep trouble, too. What the Atkinsons need right now is an informed adviser who can sit them down and straighten them out.

To put it simply, the Atkinsons have been living beyond their means. Despite that nice $12,800-a-year salary, they have been spending more than they have been making, and saving nothing. In short, the Atkinson family finances have gotten out of control.

It isn't that they are wastrels or spendthrifts, it's just that they don't know enough about financial planning—and what they do know is largely misinformation. For example, they don't keep a budget because Jeff read somewhere that paying bills by check would provide him with a ready-made budget. If he wants to know how much they spent on transportation last month, he thinks that all he has to do is look at the canceled check for the garage bill. No one has told him that in effect he has been putting a very creaky cart before a sick horse.

And there's Phoebe, who believes she knows all about rent. She read somewhere that monthly rent payments should not exceed the equivalent of one week's salary. So when the ad for their apartment, asking "$240 mo.," appeared in the newspaper, she rushed right over and grabbed it. After all, Jeff did make more than $240 a week, didn't he? No one had told her that the rule of   13 thumb was meant to apply to disposable or *after-tax take-home income*, not gross income.

The Atkinsons might have realized earlier that they were driving without a steering wheel if it had not been for the "Swift Credit" plan whereby Jeff was able to overdraw his checking account. Whatever he used, he could pay back in monthly installments—plus, of course, "a small charge on the outstanding balance each month for the use of this money."

A warning sign

Jeff should have known that something was wrong with his financial situation when he applied for the full $5,000 "Swift Credit" line but was turned down. However, he did get $1,200—just enough, it turned out, to mask the fact that the Atkinsons' monthly expenditures were exceeding their income.

If the Atkinsons had kept a budget, this is how it would have looked:

MONTHLY INCOME

$900 (Jeff's salary after withholding taxes and other payroll deductions)

Monthly Expenses

Rent $240
Auto ....$100 *(garage, gas, oil, repairs)*
Clothing $110
Food $220
*Living $310
_____
Total $980

*(including utilities, telephone, recreation, medical, tobacco, liquor, etc.)

Monthly credit payments:

Auto ....$ 70
Color television ....$ 16
Swift Credit ....$ 18
Personal loan ....$ 68
Charge accounts ....$ 33
                           $ 205

Total monthly expenditures $1,185
Less monthly income ....$ 900

Average monthly deficit ....$ 285

But to see the true dimensions of their problem would
have required the preparation of this cash balance sheet:

LIQUID ASSETS

Cash on
    hand $23
Bank ......$11   (checking account
                              balance)

Total $34

LIABILITIES

Charge accounts ....$ 339
Auto $1,500
Personal loan ....$ 880
Swift Credit $1,200
Color television ....$ 320

Total liabilities $4,239
Minus liquid assets...........$ 34

Net amount owed $4,205   15

Question: How did the Atkinsons get into this mess?
Answer: A lack of knowledge, discipline and control in managing their family finances. *Overspending*.

The stimulus to spend

A recent report, *Advertising—A Consumer View*, in the Harvard Press indicates that each day the average individual in a family gets "a message" from about 80 different advertisements from print and audio-visual media. Most of these are strongly designed to promote consumer spending. On an annual basis, advertisers themselves are spending almost $20 billion to stimulate the appetites of consumers for their products and services.

Some of this advertising is simple and forthright. A department store ad in your daily newspaper for a January white sale, for example, is usually a matter-of-fact announcement. The housewife reacts to it on a fairly logical basis; if she needs linens, the "sale" ad may prompt her to buy some; if not, she lets the sale go by.

No one will question the contribution such direct advertising makes to our economic growth. For the most part, the expenditure of some $20 billion annually in advertising involves a presentation of needed goods and services that are offered to the consumer.

But there is another kind of stimulus that is more subtle.

"The use of mass psychoanalysis to guide campaigns of persuasion has become the basis of a multimillion dollar industry," Vance Packard has written in *The Hidden Persuaders*. "The sale to us of billions of dollars' worth of products is being significantly affected."

The Atkinsons (and millions of families in the same predicament) are a case in point. For example, why did they invest all that extra money in a new station wagon— with its extra costs to purchase, operate, maintain and insure—when they could have bought a perfectly adequate smaller auto at a significant all around saving to them?

Prestige, probably. That shiny new station wagon was a status symbol which the Atkinsons at first desired and later felt they actually needed. And the Atkinsons can be expected to trade in their new station wagon in a few years, too, not because it will be physically obsolete, but because it will be psychologically obsolete. Auto merchandisers have become highly successful in making people almost ashamed of driving a car that is more than three or four years old. And this strategy has been extended to cover refrigerators, stoves, TV sets, clothes, luggage—just about everything the family uses.

But this is only one side of the two-edged sword that makes financial independence so difficult to achieve. The other edge: the many forms of credit that make overspending and overconsumption so easy.

Committing your future income

"Fly now! Pay later."

"For only a few cents a day, you can enjoy big-picture color television in your own home!"

"Need money? See Mr. Blanford, our yes-man in the personal loan department!"

"No need to spend a long, hot summer. Easy payment terms arranged for our full line of air conditioners!"

Such lures surround the family on all sides. The availability and the use of credit have become so commonplace that the present generation would find it difficult to believe that buy-now-pay-later was regarded as anything but routine not too long ago.

There's nothing wrong with using credit—when it is used wisely, meaning when you can afford it and when the credit purchase represents a genuine (as opposed to synthetic) need.

The wise use of credit is, some economists say, a form of future savings in that the consumer acquires and uses something today for which he pays by allocating part of his future income. Financial institutions have labored to help us fill our sensible credit needs, and today credit plans exist in all sizes, shapes and descriptions.

Savings banks are one of the least expensive sources of consumer credit in the 11 states where they have legislative authority to provide this customer service. In all 18 states they also provide low-cost passbook or personal savings loans—but more about these later on.

The problem most families face is that the use of credit has become so widespread, the ways of using it so numerous (there are installment sales plans, revolving charge accounts, regular charge accounts, the all-purpose credit card), that often caution and discretion are thrown to the winds. And here the danger lies: the credit trap.

Like our friends the Atkinsons, millions of families have become so indiscriminate in their use of buy-now-pay-later plans that they are merely spinning their wheels in the effort to get ahead. The average family committed to credit plans today is forced to allocate more than 25 percent of after-tax income to cover installment payment charges. If we were to lump the various forms of long- and short-term consumer debts together, the total would be well in excess of $300 billion—more than $5,000 for every family in America.

Warning! Borrow only when necessary and only when you can afford it.

The easy-money talk that bombards our ears and eyes from all sides omits mention of one financial fact of life: what you borrow or buy on credit today represents cash you must repay tomorrow. If your standard of living is based on credit, you are living dangerously since you have already spent tomorrow's income—and the piper must be paid. Each year more than 100,000 families go bankrupt.

To the family that overborrows to overspend, financial independence will never be more than an idle dream.

Financial independence—what it means

Is financial independence to be achieved only through a life of privation—a self-denial whereby we forgo all the good things in life in order to accumulate money and property we may never enjoy?

Not at all.

Financial independence should not be regarded as some distant goal in life, but rather as *a way of life*. The family that exercises reasonable care in managing its money, and common sense in its financial planning, can achieve freedom from chronic monetary anxieties and still enjoy the major benefits and advantages of our highly affluent society.

But like everything else worthwhile in life, financial independence requires an effort—and it is a continuing effort that must be woven into the whole fabric of the family's existence.

The basic elements of family financial independence are knowledge, discipline and control—a lack of which, as we have seen, backed the Atkinsons into a corner.

Knowledge means teaching ourselves to distinguish among *imperatives, needs* and *desires*.

Imperatives are the things a family *must* have to perpetuate its existence—food, shelter, clothing.

Needs include health protection and financial protection, education and recreation—the things the family *ought* to have to protect and improve its way of life.

Desires represent all the comforts and luxuries the family may *want* to have but does not really need—the things we seek to indulge ourselves or to use as status symbols in order to keep up with or outpace the family next door.

Discipline means establishing priorities and maintaining a sensible balance between imperatives, needs and desires. It means not yielding to the cult of overconsumption. It means making our own value judgments and sticking to them.

Control means allocating our family income, saving and expenditures to conform with the priorities we establish in our family financial planning.

There are two operative words in that last sentence— *saving* and *planning*.

Up to now, very little has been said about saving, not because it is unimportant but because it is so important that in order to get at the subject properly it has been necessary first to clear away some of the underbrush and overgrowth surrounding it. As we intend to show, the key to all successful financial planning is a savings program, both in the life of a business firm and in the life of a family.

For the family is a growing organism with a life apart from the lives of its members. The lives of any of its members begin in the cradle. But the life of a family begins at the altar and begins to end with retirement. In between the family grows from nascence through adolescence to maturity, and its financial requirements undergo significant changes in the process.

Thus, to gain financial independence, the family needs *planning* rather than merely a financial plan. To produce the best results, planning will be dynamic rather than static —changing as the family's financial needs change over the life cycle of the family.

Knowledge, discipline, control—the essential elements of financial independence.

Planning and saving—the essential actions.

HOW TO HAVE AN EXTRA $5,000 NEXT YEAR

A home, education for the children, a financial "cushion"—these are the goals of most married people, but every couple tailors its way of spending money to meet individual needs. Even when your best friends have the same desires you have, their spending priorities are probably very different from yours. The important thing is that you see eye to eye with your mate, that you agree on how the family income is to be used. With thought—and once you agree—you can arrive at an intelligent plan that works. There is very seldom any family disagreement over saving money at a high-dividend paying mutual savings bank.

If a young wife works and deposits the major portion of her weekly take-home earnings (say $70) into a savings bank account, while her husband adds $25 of his take-home salary to the same account each week, look what happens at the end of one year: the combined deposits—$95 each week—total up to $4,940. Add to this the regular interest dividends your savings bank pays—and you have a plus–$5,000 "cushion." One year. Think about it . . . .

Chapter Two

Money Wisdom Starts in Childhood

The seeds of family financial wisdom cannot be planted too early in life. Children who begin to learn about money management in their early years and continue these lessons through adolescence will be several light-years ahead of their untutored peers by the time they are ready for marriage.

Since there is practically nothing taught in most elementary and secondary schools about family money management, the teaching of this subject must be a family responsibility. All you need to start young children off in the right direction is a stack of pennies. In terms of learning about money management, a penny earned is literally worth its weight in gold.

Children, as part of the family circle, should make routine contributions to the family's well-being, just as the family will make routine contributions (usually in the form of small regular allowances) to their well-being. They should not get rewards for doing what is expected of them around the house—straightening their rooms, for instance. But when they are asked to perform extra services, they should receive extra compensation above and beyond the normal allowance. If the son is assigned the weekly chore of mowing the lawn, he may get something extra for it. If the daughter is in charge of washing the dog, she may get something extra, too.

Give children additional things to do and pay them little "salaries"—and they'll love it.

You can't begin too early to teach them how to save. Children accept fairies, witches, angels, Santa Claus, Batman and monsters without seeing them, but this does not apply to most other things. Thus, while there is much to be said for the usual piggy banks as a convenient repository for children's savings, a plain glass jar may be just as good. Cut a slit in the cover of the jar and screw it on so tight that it will be beyond the boy's—or his sister's—strength to unscrew it. Then they can watch their savings grow as the coins pile up. This might give them more incentive to save than would a metallic bank that hides their savings from view.

When you pay Johnny for his extra services and he slips in the coins, add a few cents now and then for interest. He'll get the idea in a jiffy. Teach Janie the value of money by taking her to the store now and then and letting her spend some of her own money on something she may want.

One family taught its four children how to count, add and subtract by keeping track of coins in their savings jars—before each of the children was five years old. By the time they were six, they knew all about nickels, dimes, quarters, half-dollars and dollars, too.

There's no limit to what children can learn about money at home—if you'll take the trouble to teach them. Psychologists hold that the educational influence of the family environment is a more powerful instructive force than the formal lessons taught in school.

CHILD'S BUDGET

Income	Weekly
Allowance	
Earnings	
Gifts	
Other	

Expenses	Weekly
Savings	
Refreshments (candy, ice cream, soda, hamburgers, etc.)	
Carfare	
Books	
Records	
Gifts	
Toys, games	
Movies	
Rides	
Other	

List of Special Things to Save For
Baseball glove
Doll clothes
Record album
Other

TEEN-AGER'S WEEKLY BUDGET

Income	Weekly
Allowance	
Part-time work	
Gifts	
Other	

Expenses	Weekly
Savings	
School supplies	
Lunches	
Carfare	
Other	

Things I Should Have and Will Save to Buy	
New bike	
Ice skates	
Other	

What I'd like to Have and Will Save to Buy	
Record player	
Guitar	
Other	

Money lessons during school years

The earning-saving-spending lessons that children learn in preschool years can be expanded as the youngsters proceed through elementary school. As soon as they have enough knowledge of the three R's, they can be introduced to budget-keeping.

Of course their first budgets will be simple—merely a record of their earnings, savings and spending, in the form of simple entries in a copybook. But give Johnny a special book (better still, let him use his savings to buy it), have him label it clearly for what it is—"Johnny's Budget"—and don't let him use it for anything else.

The first entries in the savings column of Johnny's budget may be the cash gifts he received at birth from relatives or friends—gifts that wise parents will have deposited in a savings bank account for him. Many savings banks offer a school savings program in their communities. These programs all work essentially the same way: children make deposits systematically at school, and the amounts are duly recorded in their name by the savings bank.

But don't let participation in a school savings program eliminate the youngster's "budget book." School savings should be just one important part of his complete record of earning, saving and spending activities.

Higher finance in high school

By the time children reach adolescence and head for high school they are ready to add a new dimension to their simple budgets—planning. A *budget* is essentially a monthly record of income and what has and is being spent. It becomes part of an overall *financial plan*, however, when goals are set and when earning, saving and spending practices are controlled in order to fulfill these goals.

It is in high school that young people begin to get

concerned with the course their lives will take later on. Their decisions, reached with the help of parental guidance, will in turn have impact on the family's own financial planning.

It goes without saying that a college education is probably essential if a person is going to have the best career opportunities in later life. A high school student who goes to work immediately after graduation will be mighty lucky if he comes up with a job that pays $400 a month to start. Compare this with the average monthly *starting* salaries for graduates with bachelor's and master's degrees, as compiled recently by Northwestern University:

OCCUPATION	B.A.	M.A.
Business administration	$550	$709
Production management	591	687
Chemistry	607	724
Sales—marketing	549	728
Physics	620	725
Accounting	579	693
Math—statistics	562	719
Engineering	662	775
Liberal arts	541	670
Economics—finance	574	720
Other occupations	543	722

The differences in total earnings of non-college men and college graduates usually become even greater later on. The *lifetime income* of the non-college man will, on the average, be only about one-third of the total income earned by the college graduate. It may be as little as one-quarter of the total income of the graduate who goes on to take his master's. So a postgraduate degree opens the door to a solid career opportunity in almost any field.

Is the demand for those with a master's degree high? A recent study by the University of Michigan showed that during a three-month winter period some 380 companies

27

sent talent scouts to hold on-campus interviews. They offered jobs to 200 postgraduate students who expected to get their master's degrees from the University's Graduate School of Business Administration the following spring. All the job offers carried starting salaries in the ranges listed above.

But a college education costs money—an ever-increasing amount. Today it will take a minimum of $2,000 a year to defray tuition and on-campus living costs at the less expensive colleges. The figure easily *doubles* at the more expensive schools. And in the years ahead the cost is certain to rise further. A family should plan to allocate at least $8,000 to $10,000 for Johnny's bachelor degree and at least $12,000 to $14,000 if he goes on to take two years of postgraduate work.

Today the middle income family cannot count on college scholarships paying the way even when a youngster has top marks and qualifications for a merit scholarship. Most scholarship funds today are allocated on the basis of need and are reduced practically to nothing when the family income reaches roughly the $15,000-a-year level.

Millions of high school students these days are working part-time to help accumulate the funds for a college education. Many families open a special account in a savings bank for the specific purpose of funding at least part of the costs. Helped by the high-level interest rates that savings banks pay, the regular monthly deposits in the college account quickly mount up.

Suppose that over a four-year period—during the student's high school years—regular monthly deposits of $80 are put into a college fund savings account. The student might contribute $25 monthly from part-time wages and the family the other $55. With savings interest added, there would be well over $5,000 in the college fund by the time the student completes high school.

There seems little doubt that the costs of a college

education will continue to go up. Thus, it is almost impossible for the average family to provide for these costs out of current income, especially if more than one student is in college at the same time. Many families will discover that even a well-planned and executed college fund savings plan will leave them short of the full amount needed. Luckily, financial assistance has become available in the form of student loans.

The importance of student loans

Savings banks are leaders in the student loan field. Full student loan programs are now being implemented by savings banks in the six New England states, plus New York, New Jersey and Pennsylvania. Certain limited programs are also available among savings banks in Maryland, Indiana and Wisconsin.

The maximum amount a student may borrow will vary, depending on whether a state-guaranteed program is offered or whether the federal-guaranteed program is the sole source of financial assistance.

The federal program specifies that borrowers need not be full-time students, but they must be at least half-time students at institutions of higher learning accredited by the Commissioner of Education. The program is limited to U.S. nationals or permanent residents in this country. Families whose adjusted income exceeds $15,000 are not eligible.

The loan is not made to the family but to the student. The borrowing student is required to present the lending institution with an affidavit from his school stating that he has been accepted for enrollment or is a student in good standing. While the student is in school, the federal government pays all interest and service charges.

The student begins to repay the loan from nine months to one year after he completes his studies—or becomes less than a half-time student. He can repay over a five-to-ten-year period, but must finish the payments within 15 years after getting the loan. When the student begins repayment of his loan, the federal government's interest payments cease.

The young budgeteers

Thus youngsters in their high school years, through part-time work that builds a fund to help defray their college costs, and by learning how a savings bank student loan can bridge the remaining gap, actually take part in the family financial planning.

The high school years are also an ideal time to begin teaching young people how to set up and manage a budget in conjunction with the family's short-, medium- and long-term goals. A high school student in his junior and senior years might be taught how to write checks for bill-paying by preparing them for parental signature, and he can be taught how to balance the checkbook when the bank statement arrives.

By the same token, a girl should take her turn at managing the family budget and checkbook during her high school years. Recent studies show that in eight out of ten cases the housewife fills the role of family comptroller.

Girls can lend real assistance to their mothers in meeting the family's continuing need for one of the budget's biggest items—food. Even a careful family may spend more than $1,500 a year for food. The time to begin teaching girls how to stretch food dollars and keep these expenditures in line with the budget is when they are young.

After a girl has accompanied her mother to the supermarket a few times and has learned the melon-choosing, economy-size buying tricks—to name but a few —give her a chance to make out the family shopping list and do the shopping on her own. The most important thing to teach her is that the overall family budget, rather than impulse buying, must be the controlling factor in determining how much she spends, and on what.

Youngsters who may have developed valuable saving habits through school savings plans at the elementary school level will often discard them in high school unless they are given new incentives to practice thrift. There's nothing more satisfying to parents than giving things to their children—but in the long run one of the greatest gifts is the practice of thrift and self-reliance. So when John wants nothing more in life than a motor bike—or when Jane hungers for that new pair of skis and you'd like to give it to her—try this technique: encourage the youngster to save the amount needed, then buy the article desired and present it as a gift, giving the youngster the right to deposit the accumulated funds in his or her savings account.

Priorities in college

College students usually have ample opportunity to earn money in part-time jobs after classes, but the wise family will make certain that sons and daughters put first things first—in this case, the good marks that go with learning. Job recruiters have made it clear that the better the student's grades, the better the chances of getting the top jobs available after graduation.

Some families will insist that John and Jane test the scholastic climate during their freshman year by devoting all their time to their books. This enables them to bring back a realistic report of the time they can give to part-time work without impeding their studies during the remaining years.

Still, the college years are an excellent time to transfer real financial responsibilities to young people's shoulders. Instead of merely sending off checks each month to cover John's or Jane's expenses, let them open their own checking accounts at this time and manage their own budgets.

Make sure they continue to develop the habit of saving during the college years. If necessary, give them a reason, a goal. Here's how one young woman was given the incentive to continue her savings in college (and also motivated not to drop out before she had her degree). Her father told her as she began her junior year that he would give her, as a graduation present, half the cost of a trip to Europe. She would have to save the other half. With this target, she was able to put aside $500 in savings during her last two years of college, which her father matched as promised on graduation day.

HOW TO ENCOURAGE YOUR CHILDREN TO SAVE

Take your children along when you do your banking. Let them put their savings into their own mutual savings bank account. Ten dimes from a piggy bank, or 100 pennies carefully saved in a jar or little box (or even in an old marble bag), will open a savings account for a child. Your mutual savings bank's friendliness and interest in young savers will encourage your children as they begin to build the habit of saving at an early age.

The lessons your children learn from having a savings account of their own, and by going along when you do your own banking, will be invaluable to them throughout their lives. They will learn, for example, not to spend their allowance money as fast as they get it, and they'll soon see that money in a savings bank account is at work, growing for them all the time.

So when your children ask, "Take me along to the savings bank with you," do it!

Chapter Three

When You're Young and Single

The vast majority of young people can expect to spend at least one or two post-college years in self-supporting employment before they get married and start families of their own, according to many sociological studies.

During these swinging years—the first years of independence before responsibilities set in—young people run a serious risk of throwing their early good saving habits to the winds. Many young and single people, once they begin earning their own incomes, actually become dissavers: they spend all and often more than they earn. Clothes, cars, vacations, entertainment, meals—they all can be had on a buy-now-pay-later plan.

But what often gets a young person into trouble is the fact that tomorrow *does* come, and you *do* have to pay later. If you fall into the habit of living beyond your income before marriage, you probably are not going to change overnight just because the wedding bells have rung. Put two such young people together—and a marriage is off to a shaky start.

Does this mean you should forgo all use of credit

when you are single? Not at all; just don't go overboard—keep your head even though others about you may be losing theirs.

Money and the single man

In reality, these single years can be an excellent training period for learning how to use credit wisely and well. There are two simple rules (unfortunately, more often honored in the breach rather than the observance): (1) don't borrow what you can't afford to pay back; (2) shop for the best credit terms you can get.

No simple formula can be instantly applied to determine the amount of one's borrowing limit. Obviously it is unwise to go out on a limb before you've put something aside to tide you over in case of an emergency—accident, illness, unemployment and the like. And if you're planning to get married someday, you'll need funds to finance that happy event. So start building your savings with that first paycheck and make your savings allocation out of each paycheck your first order of business. That way—and only that way—you'll give the practice of thrift the top priority it deserves in planning and managing your financial affairs.

A second necessary early step to determine your borrowing limit will be budgeting the remainder of your paycheck against the recurring demands that will be made on it. More often than not, the post-college young man or woman takes up "co-op" living. This usually means either living at home and contributing a share of one's earnings to the family's overall income or sharing new living quarters away from home with other young people.

In either case, you'll have to allocate part of your paycheck to cover your share of rent, food and other such apportioned costs. You'll also have recurring personal expenses—carfare or commutation fare, dry-cleaning, recreation, toiletries and at least a dozen more. These should be written into your budget as standard deductions before you decide how much of your income can be safely used to finance any buy-now-pay-later commitments.

All this means that your borrowing limit is the amount you can afford to allocate from your paychecks *after* you have taken care of your savings needs and your living expenses. Whether you are paid weekly, biweekly or monthly, you should compute this on a monthly basis.

Let's assume, for example, that a young man's monthly take-home pay is $600 after deductions for taxes, medical insurance, social security and similar items. Since he is a marriage-minded young man, he will probably want to allocate at least 20 percent for savings, or $120. If he budgets $350 to cover his living expenses, he will have about $130 remaining. Certainly he'll be wise to restrict his credit purchases to a level that will not require more than $130 each month for total installment repayments.

Credit costs vary

He also demonstrates financial wisdom by choosing the least expensive form of credit available. Let us say that our young man moves into an unfurnished apartment together with a former college roommate and they decide to spend $600 each for furniture. They can get this $1,200 in credit in many ways. They can open a charge account in a department store. They can borrow the money directly from a personal finance company. They can borrow it from a commercial bank. Or, if they are fortunate enough to live in a savings bank state, they can borrow it as a savings bank consumer loan or a personal savings passbook loan.

Does it make a difference *where* they get it? Definitely.

The use of that $1,200 in credit for one year can cost them as little as $72 or as much as $216 or more, depending on *how and where* they borrow it. A passbook loan or personal savings loan at a savings bank that costs 6 percent in terms of true annual interest, for example, would mean

35

a $72 credit cost. On the other end of the scale would be the almost 32 percent they could pay if the charge is 1½ percent per month of the initial $1,200 purchase price for their furniture.

So choosing the right form of credit can itself be a form of saving. If it costs about $72 for a $1,200 passbook loan at a savings bank versus $216 or more for $1,200 in credit from some other source, the difference is a saving of at least $144 to the borrower.

One problem young borrowers have faced in the past was the mathematical chore of figuring out in terms of true annual interest just how much each type of credit costs. You can use a simple "multiply-by-two" formula to convert discount rates into their rough equivalent of true annual interest.

For example, take one low-cost form of installment loan offered by mutual savings banks. A savings bank passbook loan described as $3.33 per $100 discount bears a true annual interest charge of 6.30 percent over one year although the effective cost to the borrower is reduced by the interest he continues to earn on the full balance in his savings account. Unsecured consumer loans, which are offered by savings banks in some states, may cost somewhat more, but these rates usually are below those charged by commercial banks and other lenders who also quote their rates at a discount.

In 1968, a federal Truth-in-Lending law was passed. Upon becoming fully operative it enables borrowers to tell at a glance how much they are asked to pay for credit. The law requires lenders to state the cost of credit in terms of both the true annual interest rate percentage and the dollar cost over the life of the loan.

However, in many of our states, "truth-in-lending" protection is not new. Borrowers here have had similar protection for some time under state "truth" laws.

HOW YOUR REGULAR SAVINGS GROW

(Calculated at 5% interest; compounded quarterly)

How Much You Will Have on Deposit
at the End of . . .

Save This Much Weekly	1 Year	2 Years	5 Years	10 Years	20 Years
$ 5	$ 266.74	$ 547.07	$1,476.69	$ 3,369.88	$ 8,908.68
$10	533.48	1,094.14	2,953.39	6,739.76	17,817.37
$15	800.22	1,641.21	4,430.09	10,109.64	26,726.06
$20	1,066.96	2,188.28	5,906.79	13,479.53	35,634.75
$25	1,333.70	2,735.35	7,383.49	16,849.41	44,543.44

How to finance your wedding

Young people who intend to get married will be most unwise to involve themselves in long-term credit commitments that cannot be liquidated in a year or less. The same policy of "no entangling alliances" should prevail if you share an apartment with a friend and both of you sign the lease. Try to get a lease with a clause permitting either of you to sublet and also be sure you have a mutual agreement, in writing, that in the event of marriage the obligations of the old lease don't follow you up the middle aisle.

You are also wise to incorporate similar escape clauses in any credit commitment you share with your temporary living partner. No one knows when Dan Cupid will strike; you may want to terminate all past commitments quickly and easily.

When the right person for you comes along, your focus will shift dramatically to marriage planning. The first order of business will be the financing of your wedding. Few young people realize how much it costs these days to get married. Fewer are fully aware of the huge expenditures that will be required soon after the wedding. Consider these statistics about the almost two million marriages in the United States during one year—1968:

About $500 million was spent on engagement and wedding rings.

About $8 billion was spent on wedding purchases including clothes, reception food and drink and wedding shower and gifts, but *not* including such post-wedding expenditures as honeymoons, furniture, appliances, apartments and the other must expenses for setting up a new home.

Post-wedding expenses *during the first year* following those marriages were estimated as totaling at least $3 billion more.

Traditionally, the bride's family pays the $1,000 to $1,500 that the average wedding costs. A typical list of relatively modest expenses would include:

Wedding gown (and accessories)	*$250*
Invitations, postage	*100*
Church fees and decorations	*200*
Flowers	*125*
Transportation (to and from church)	*75*
Photographs	*80*
Bridesmaids' luncheon	*25*
Reception (food, drink, catering)	*150*
Bride's gift to groom	*40*
Hotel rooms for attendants	*40*
Gratuities	*80*
Miscellaneous	*100*
Total	*$1,265*

Plan for your honeymoon—and after

While the father of the bride is traditionally expected to keep his checkbook handy to cover a major share of the wedding costs, the groom by no means escapes free. Besides the wedding and engagement rings, he pays for the blood tests, marriage license, the rental of formal clothes for himself and the male attendants, gratuities for the clergy and altar attendants, the bride's bouquet and present and gifts for male attendants.

Not to mention the cost of the honeymoon.

The bride, of course, is expected to provide her trousseau—and considering the costs of women's clothes and linen these days, the demands on her finances are hardly less stringent than those faced by the groom.

Thus the costs a young couple will have to defray for their wedding and honeymoon are likely to run between $2,000 and $3,000. A young man or young woman is wise to begin saving toward this end as soon as he or she begins working, even though plans for any marriage have not yet materialized. If both individuals accumulate enough savings to cover their individual wedding expenses, they will be ideally set to save together during their engagement period, building a fund against the heavy expenditures needed to start a new home after their honeymoon.

You can expect outlays for apartment rent, utility down payments, furniture and appliances and so on to total at least $2,000 during the first year of marriage. So don't be afraid to take advantage of your parents, if you have a chance, to indicate that you have a preference for the "ideal" marriage gift—*money*. Newlyweds who receive cash—or the equivalent of cash in the form of accounts opened in a savings bank in their name—can save or spend these funds to fulfill their first financial plan and budget.

Incidentally, the best time to think about your financial plan and family budget is before, rather than after, the wedding. A savings bank is an excellent place to gather information and get counseling for planning and budgeting, even though you may want to postpone formalizing a budget until you have returned from your honeymoon.

Chapter Four

When You're Young and Married

One of the more common, and serious, mistakes of young married people with regard to money management is to set up a family budget without first deciding on long-term financial goals. It is like rushing to the microscope, when what you really need first is a telescope.

Let us take sensible young Jim Doubleton and his wife, Julia, as an example. They have just returned from their honeymoon with stars in their eyes and the sincere desire to use common sense in managing their financial affairs. An intelligent young couple, they know that no one can see around all the turns in the road ahead or solve all the problems and challenges of life before they arrive. But they know, too, that "problems anticipated are problems half-solved."

They have decided they are going to enjoy what family life is all about—having children. They assume that their first child will probably be along in a year or so, and they would like the second to arrive a year or two later.

41

The cost of togetherness

Jim is now 25, Julia is 23. Jim has a take-home pay of $7,500 a year after taxes and other payroll deductions; Julia's take-home pay is $5,500.

They don't want to fall into the trap of starting married life on a double income standard and then having to fall back on a single income when Julia becomes pregnant and wishes to stop working. They have accumulated about $2,000 in savings during their engagement period, to defray some of the heavy costs of their first marriage year. But they know they should have additional liquid savings for unforeseeable needs or emergencies, so they decide now that while Julia continues to work they will deposit her take-home pay in a savings bank account.

So far, so good.

They next decide that setting up a new household is complicated enough without the added burdens that come with buying a house—even if they could afford it. They believe, however, that there are advantages to raising children in the suburbs or exurbs. So they agree: "Some day we'll buy a house," deciding to put off the home-buying plans until some future date.

That's where they've made their first mistake.

This is a mistake young people commonly make— they assume they are planning for the future by sweeping the future behind them. Actually, as soon as the Doubletons decided they were going to buy a house, they set themselves a long-term goal. If they are to fulfill this goal, they will need a long-term plan to achieve it.

The Doubletons agree, too, that life insurance protection is basic to a family's security, but they reason that since Jim's company provides him with life coverage under a group plan, they can postpone planning their own insurance program "until later on."

Another mistake. Adequate insurance coverage for the Doubleton family will change as time goes on. They will have to review their insurance plan periodically through the years. It is something they should consider fully at the earliest possible time since the younger a person's age when he buys insurance, the lower the premium costs. Also, Julia's status as a beneficiary will change radically when they start to raise a family.

The Doubletons agree, too, that they will have to put something aside for their children's education, and once more they put this expenditure into the background as "something we will deal with when the time comes."

Once more they have made a mistake. They have set another long-term goal, but without making a long-term plan.

Next, they discuss retirement. They know they will need some form of income when Jim's working days end, and that company retirement plans do not meet these needs fully. But since Jim won't reach retirement age for another 40 years, they think—well, there's plenty of time to plan for that later on. . . .

Again they have erred; they have set another long-term goal without a long-term plan.

Planning is the answer

Are we saying that Jim and Julia should immediately start saving out of income to cover, simultaneously, the cost of buying a house, adequate lifetime insurance protection, educating their children and financing their retirement?

The question answers itself—it would be ridiculous. But it is almost as ridiculous to assume that these financial needs will take care of themselves without planning.

Take the matter of insurance. Instead of the "later on" approach, let us assume the Doubletons decide that once Julia leaves her job to become a mother and housewife, they will begin to build around the group coverage provided by Jim's employer. An excellent start. Even

43

though they are not actually doing something about an important element of their progress toward financial independence, they have firmly established the starting point.

The young married couple, using a telescope in their financial planning, should establish a point in time for beginning each of their long-term goals, if the goals are to become a reality.

For the Doubletons, this also means finding the point in time when, assuming their children arrive on schedule, they want a home of their own. When children reach school age, they usually become involved for the first time in the serious business of making friends. If the Doubletons were to delay buying a house until their children were well along in primary school, it might mean submitting their children to the disconcerting experience of an unfamiliar school system with different teaching methods and emphasis, and also disrupting important friendships.

So the Doubletons decide an ideal time for moving into their own house (probably in a new neighborhood) would be about seven years from now. The first entry on their long-term financial plan becomes:

LONG-TERM GOAL	TARGET DATE
Buying a house	*Seven years*

Training their telescope even further into the future, they now establish the time for their second long-term goal—the advanced education of their two children. If the first arrives on schedule the college years will begin in about 18 years. So they establish a second date on their long-term plan:

College education ....18 years

Their third long-range target will be retirement, which will begin in about 40 years. Their long-term goals then will appear in this sequence:

LONG-TERM GOAL	TARGET DATE
Buying a house..........*Seven years*	
College education ....*18 years*	
Retirement ....*40 years*	

Now the Doubletons must cope with the financial implications of this picture.

Working plans to meet long-term goals

The Doubletons begin their financial planning by first establishing how much cash they will need in seven years for home-buying.

How much should they pay for it?

Realizing that in this era of continuous population explosion there is no better asset than real estate, they decide to spend as much as they can afford. But they don't want to go overboard and buy too much house. They limit their planned investment to a formula of three times Jim's disposable income. But the figure they are after is three times Jim's disposable income in seven years, so they do some estimating. They assume his salary will increase at an annual rate of approximately 5 percent, meaning that his take-home pay then will be about $11,000 annually.

Their long-term financial plan begins to take shape: in seven years they will be looking for a house costing about $33,000. Next consideration: how much cash will they need to achieve this goal?

A 20 percent down payment means $6,600. Closing costs and moving expenses—$1,000 more. Total amount of home-buying cash needed: $7,600.

Now they do some arithmetic: if they put $81 a month into a mutual savings bank account for 84 months and add the bank's current level of interest payments to their funds, they will easily hit their $7,600 target in seven years.

Thus the first long-range element of their financial   45

plan comes into focus: they need a savings rate of $81 each month, equal to 13 percent of Jim's current monthly take-home pay of $625, which should enable them to achieve their first long-range goal—a home in seven years.

Note that they plan to make this allocation *before* they begin figuring out their monthly budget. In effect, the Doubletons have not swept their future behind them as many young couples are prone to do; instead they have a clear picture of where they want to be seven years later and have plotted their financial course to get there.

HOW YOUR REGULAR SAVINGS GROW

(Calculated at 4¾% interest; compounded quarterly)

How Much You Will Have on Deposit at the End of ...

Save This Much Weekly	1 Year	2 Years	5 Years	10 Years	20 Years
$ 5	$ 266.36	$ 545.60	$1,466.98	$ 3,324.63	$ 8,655.76
$10	532.72	1,091.21	2,933.97	6,649.27	17,311.52
$15	799.08	1,636.81	4,400.96	9,973.91	25,967.29
$20	1,065.45	2,182.42	5,867.95	13,298.54	34,623.05
$25	1,331.81	2,728.02	7,334.93	16,623.18	43.278.81

Medium-term planning

The Doubletons now take a different look at their income position. Remember, they have decided to use Julia's take-home pay in her pre-pregnancy working period to establish a liquid savings cushion for emergencies or unforeseen cash needs—a wise decision indeed. This means their anticipated real income will be Jim's paycheck. And Jim's present disposable income will be reduced by $81 each month in accordance with their long-term plan to

46

buy a house within seven years: $625 minus $81 leaves $544.

Many young couples at this point would simply budget the $544 on a month-to-month basis and feel they had done enough planning. But let us assume the Doubletons are exceptional; what they want is the best plan.

They realize that when they buy their house seven years from now, they will have to furnish it beyond their present requirements. So they decide to start now to allocate part of their $544 a month for it. They think they can manage to set aside $50 monthly, which will enable them to accumulate over the years good things of lasting value —a solid bedroom set, attractive and durable living room furniture and other items.

So before preparing their month-to-month budget, the Doubletons structure a medium-term element into their financial plan—a monthly allocation of $50 for basic purchases. This further reduces their present usable income from $544 to $494.

Are they ready to prepare the family budget?

Not quite—although a less exceptional couple might be. The Doubletons now take into account their imperative *short-term needs*—the cost of the baby they hope to have, for one thing: $300? (Fortunately these costs can be held to a minimum because Jim's employer provides him with comprehensive hospitalization and major medical insurance.) If they want to accumulate $300 during their first year of marriage, it entails setting aside an additional $25 each month, and this will mean a further reduction of their current working income figure—from $494 to $469 —the figure they now use as the basis for preparing their monthly budget.

Let us recapitulate and see what sort of financial plan the Doubletons have come up with. They have decided to live on just one income—Jim's—and:

Allocate 13 percent of $625 each month, or $81, as *long-term* savings for buying their house.

Set aside 8 percent of $625 each month, or $50, as *medium-term* savings in order to make the basic purchases needed to set up a household.

Earmark 4 percent of $625 each month, or $25, to pay for *short-term* (less than one year) expenditures—the first of which will involve a baby.

It adds up to a total savings rate of $156 each month, or 25 percent of $625.

Misleading statistics

Obviously, the Doubletons' rate of saving is much higher than the 5 to 8 percent rate which, the statistics indicate, is the average savings rate for all U.S. families. Beware the statistics! They may comfort the families that undersave; they are perilous for families intent on gaining financial independence.

In reality, there are three types of families: those with adequate savings, those that don't save enough and those that don't save at all—such as the Atkinsons mentioned in Chapter One. The Atkinsons, and millions of families like them, are what the economists call "dissavers"—families whose finances are in deficit. All three family types are lumped together to form the statistical average savings rate of 5 to 8 percent.

Families with adequate savings programs do manage to save at the rate of about 25 percent. These families, like our friends the Doubletons, begin saving toward established goals early in their marriage and then make it a lifelong practice. They achieve financial independence.

"Financial independence first of all must be a family decision and a family dedication," one financial counselor has said. "It is at once a goal in life and a way of life. It requires a continuing effort, but the rewards are immeasurable."

The time to prepare for the future is *now*. The Doubletons, by establishing a savings practice that will enable them to allocate 13 percent of Jim's current income toward the purchase of their house, have substituted planning for wishful thinking. They will also have the cushion of liquid savings built up from Julia's paychecks during the year or so she expects to work.

Equally important, they have introduced discipline into the management of their family finances. In seven years they not only will have a house they can call their own, they will also have become accustomed to saving on a long-term basis. This skill will enable them, as we shall see, to come to grips effectively with the other long-term goals on their horizon—adequate insurance protection, the cost of educating their children and the additional income needed for retirement.

HOW TO GET HELP IN PUTTING THEM THROUGH COLLEGE

You have only two children—that isn't a large family. But those college costs are zooming—up, up and away! How can you ever provide for your youngsters' higher education? Suppose you start, when each child is three years old, to put $50 a month into a mutual savings education fund—one for each child. In fifteen years—by the time each child is 18—you will have deposited $9,000 in each fund. Meanwhile, your savings bank's dividend will have added a big "bonus" regularly to each account.

To see just how much, consult the charts elsewhere in this book on "How Your Savings Grow." That's the easy way to build a solid fund that will let you underwrite those four years of college education and even, if needed, a postgraduate education. Let your savings bank help.

Chapter Five

The Maturing Family

There are many reasons why marriages break up. But grave problems with money are prominent among them. A recent study of requests for help made to family service agencies shows that more than half the couples who asked for counseling reported serious disputes over money. A recent book, *A Guide to Successful Family Living*, by the general directors of the Family Service Association of America, Clark W. Blackburn and Norman M. Lobenz, states:

"How a couple manage money can often be a key to the health of the marriage; every couple should have some kind of mutually agreed-upon plan for handling finances."

Of course, any financial plan, by its very nature, is subject to change. It can be regarded as a road map indicating the best route from coast to coast. But it cannot guarantee against the flood in Mississippi, the tornado in Kansas or the avalanche in the Rockies, all of which might necessitate a detour.

Suppose, for example, that, like the Doubletons mentioned earlier, you establish a home-buying goal several years from now and you save diligently toward that goal. But then, when you are about halfway there, a major family illness suddenly eats up half of your saved liquid assets. Obviously you have to change your financial plan. It is important that you and your spouse change it *together;* your joint planning effort will be your lifelong anchor.

Continuous planning requires that at least once each year you convene a family council to assess the financial performance of the past year and establish a new short-term plan to cover the year ahead. Of course this short-term plan will fit in with your long-term goals—home-buying, the children's education, provisions for retirement and so on. You will carry out the annual budget you set up during the planning session on a month-by-month basis.

When to hold the planning session

Some families make the mistake of trying to hold an annual planning session too early or too late in the year. For most families, the strategic time is toward the end of the year. The last week in November usually is a good time for two reasons:

Figuring your income. Most business concerns that give bonuses or reward employees with raises give out indications of what can or cannot be expected in the eleventh month. When you have this information you can develop a better estimate on the income that will be available for the year ahead.

Holding down the overspending. The average family's biggest spending splurge usually occurs in the Christmas season, and it happens every year. If the family establishes the total amount that *can* be spent just *before* the spending begins—instead of accounting afterward for how much *was* spent—you will have put up an effective "Stop" sign against impulsive overspending.

The family planning session should cover three areas: (1) your "net worth"; (2) a cash flow "projection" and (3) the best way to set up your family budget.

1. *Net worth.* This is actually a simple idea that can be defined as the amount of money the family would have left if you were to convert everything you own (all your assets) into cash and then pay off all your debts (your liabilities).

A typical net-worth statement might look like this:

NET WORTH STATEMENT
Assets

Real estate	(amount you would collect by selling your house and other real estate property)	$_____
Cash	(total amount in your savings bank accounts and checking account)	_____
Securities	(market value of your stocks, bonds, mutual fund shares and other securities)	_____
Insurance	(cash value of your life insurance policies)	_____
Automobile	(cash value of your automobile)	_____
Appliances	(cash value of washer, television set, etc.)	_____
Home furnishings	(cash value of furniture, fixtures, etc.)	_____
Other assets	(clothing, jewelry, sporting equipment, stamp collection, etc. — at market value)	_____
	Total assets	$_____

Liabilities

Long term   (debt balances that go beyond one year)

Mortgage principal (outstanding balance) $_____

Automobile loan (outstanding balance)   _____

Appliances loan (outstanding balance)   _____

Educational loan (outstanding balance)   _____

Savings bank passbook loan (outstanding balance)   _____

Insurance cash-value loan (outstanding balance)   _____

Short term   (balances to be paid within
   one year)

Department store charge accounts $_____

Other charge accounts   _____

Other installment credit   _____

Other family debts (medical, back
   taxes, etc.)   _____

   Total liabilities $_____

Your net worth (your assets minus your
   liabilities) $_____

Compare your net worth in the current year with that
of previous years at every planning season. This will give
you an excellent yardstick for measuring the soundness of
your family's money management and your progress toward achieving financial independence. For example:

NET WORTH COMPARISON
(As of November 30)

	1969	1968	1967	1966	1965	1960	1955
Total assets							
$							
Total liabilities							
Net worth $							

What rate of increase in your net worth should you
expect or be satisfied with? No percentage growth figure
will fit all families. There are too many differences between

families; also, too few statistics have been developed up to now to set up real guidelines. But many financial counselors seem to feel that a family of "average size and circumstances," if it has sound planning, saving and spending policies, will probably show an average annual increase in net worth of at least 10 percent a year, measured over a ten-year period.

A growth rate of 10 percent each year may not at all be the best rate for *your* family. Maybe it should be higher. The criterion is your success in reaching your long-term goals.

But if your net worth is not increasing each year by at least 10 percent, it may be a good idea to discuss your practices in money management with an outside adviser, and your savings banker is well qualified to fill this role. In fact, many savings banks offer a formal financial or budget counseling service.

2. *The cash flow projection.* Most businesses and corporations make an annual "cash flow projection" for the year ahead. This gives them some idea in advance of where funds will be coming from, and where they will be going, and it is vital to companies because money is what keeps the business world in business.

In family financial planning, a cash flow projection can be very helpful since it establishes the framework within which your budget will have to work.

Here is how you can draw up a simple cash flow projection for a November annual planning session:

Income	Dec.	Jan.	Feb.	Mar.	Apr.	May	June	July	Aug.	Sep.	Oct.	Nov.
Salary	$											
Bonus												
Loans												
Interest												
Other												
Total	$											

Outgo		Dec.	Jan.	Feb.	Mar.	Apr.	May	June	July	Aug.	Sep.	Oct.	Nov.
Food	$												
Shelter													
Debts													
Insurance													
Savings													
Personal													
Other													
Total	$												
Surplus	$												
or													
Deficit	$												

The cash flow projection will serve another useful purpose in that it provides you with a quick check during the year whenever you want to determine how well the family is keeping to the monthly budget.

3. *Your family budget.* All through this book we have talked about the importance of family financial planning. Your budget will now be the key tool in keeping your family locked into a steady program that takes you toward your goals. The budget is not only a record-keeping tool. It is also your vehicle for precise and specific control of the family income and how it is spent and saved.

But here is a warning about any budget: don't make it too detailed or too demanding. If a family budget is too burdensome, its fate is foreordained—it will not be followed. Balance the desirability of having complete data about your income and expenditures against the fact that the best budget is the *simplest* one that gives you the data you must have.

To keep your budget in action, forget about a blow-by-blow accounting of each day's dollars-and-cents spending. Even a weekly budget will become too much of a chore for the average family. A monthly budget will usually be best—if it is properly planned.

One of the best ways of creating a budget is to use a budget book with separate pages for each month. Savings banks and other financial institutions often make such books available to you; or you can set up your own.

No two families will include the same information in the same way in their budgets, but you should always keep your expenditures in approximate balance with income. Here is a real-life excerpt from one family's budget book.

BUDGET FOR JULY

Take-home income (after tax withholding and other payroll deductions)	$940	
Savings bank deposits	— 270	
Expendable income	670	$670
Expenditures (to the nearest dollar)		
Mortgage (including interest, amortization, taxes and insurance)	$180	
Gas & electric	12	
Telephone	11	
Heat	15	
Food	145	
House furnishings	11	
House miscellaneous	7	
Clothing	30	
Allowances	40	
Contributions	15	
Recreation, entertainment	35	
Commutation	19	
Auto (gas, oil, repairs)	30	
Insurance:		
Life	62	
Medical	8	
Auto	15	
Passbook loan repayment	40	
	675	$675
Deficit		— $ 5

The family whose budget is shown actually saved 29 percent of income and was willing to discuss its budget techniques. Here is what this interview revealed:

Savings. The family's cardinal rule was to make its savings deposits *before* it made any other allocation from a paycheck. In other words, the family paid *itself* first.

"We use three accounts," the father explained. "Our long-term account has been building steadily now for the past four years. We almost emptied it to take care of the mortgage down payment on the house in 1964, but we've been building it again ever since.

"We have another account that we use for appliances and other home improvement purposes. This account goes up and down every couple of years.

"We have a third account that we call the 'Put and Take' account. We'll be tapping this for $300 or so to cover a vacation around Labor Day. What's left we'll use for Christmas and birthday gifts."

Auto expenses. The family said its July expenditures were unusually high, causing the $5 deficit. The family car is a small station wagon, and it was used a lot in July for going to the beach. The figure for driving expenses would go down in the fall after the family returned from its vacation.

Short-term loan. This family was repaying a pass-book loan that had been made in order to buy its car the previous year.

"July was a good month for us," the mother told us. "We seldom come out so close to our target. Sometimes we're $20 or $30 over when I buy meat in quantity for the freezer. But then this will cut down our food bills later on, so we begin picking up a few dollars again. We make a point, though, of never letting our budget deficit go higher than $50 at any time."

How to figure taxes

There is hardly an end to the books that have been written about personal income taxes. Still the job of filling out income tax returns each year is painful for everyone.

And each year the income tax laws seem to become more complicated and more demanding. In some communities the taxpayers now face the demands of three governments—federal, state and city—and have to file three returns.

For the taxpayer who finds he can use the short form of the Internal Revenue Service—Form 1040A—to file his federal tax return, the complications of our tax laws should not present too much of a problem. However, if you do not qualify for the short-form return and must file your federal return using a long form—Form 1040—it is a different story.

Each year the Internal Revenue Service provides an approximately 20-page booklet of printed instructions to guide you in preparing your federal income tax return. But even with these instructions, many people find that tax return time is a struggle with many uncertainties about their calculations and how they arrived at them.

If you fit that description, this book offers you two general suggestions. First, you can get help at your local office of the Internal Revenue Service. The only drawback here is that as the April 15 deadline for filing federal income tax returns approaches, more and more taxpayers ask for help at these offices. And this can mean hours of waiting in line.

You can also seek professional tax advice from a tax accountant or lawyer, depending on your specific needs. Of course, you will have to pay a fee to a professional tax adviser. If your return is challenged by the Internal Revenue Service later on, your professional tax adviser will defend it—although in most cases this will involve an additional fee.

If you are a homeowner, there are two important tax benefits to keep in mind: your local real estate taxes and, for that matter, the total dollar amount of the interest you have paid on your mortgage loan each year. Both are deductible items.

HOW YOUR REGULAR SAVINGS GROW

(Calculated at 4¼% interest; compounded quarterly)

How Much You Will Have on Deposit
at the End of ...

Save This Much Weekly	1 Year	2 Years	5 Years	10 Years	20 Years
$ 5	$ 265.68	$ 542.84	$1,448.22	$ 3,237.33	$ 8,178.05
$10	531.37	1,085.69	2,896.45	6,474.67	16,356.10
$15	797.06	1,628.54	4,344.68	9,712.01	24,534.15
$20	1,062.74	2,171.38	5,792.90	12,949.35	32,712.21
$25	1,328.43	2,714.23	7,241.13	16,186.69	40,890.26

Chapter Six

Retirement Planning

"Planning for retirement that is 40 years off is *not* ridiculous," Jim Doubleton said to Julia, his wife. "If we're going to live in comfort after I stop working, we have to begin planning now."

"But 40 years seems so far ahead," Julia answered. "It's like planning to live on Mars. I still say it's ridiculous."

"Well, dear," Jim told her, "there are about 20 million people alive today who are 65 or older, and no doubt most of them thought it was ridiculous 40 years ago to begin planning for their retirement. But a lot of them are hard up today."

Some cold facts

The Social Security Administration has produced some chilling statistics on what is happening to people in terms of their financial security at age 65:

68 percent of nonmarried people do not have incomes sufficient to maintain a "modest but adequate" level of living

One fundamental reason why so many people fail
to achieve the financial independence they desire can be
stated simply: lack of adequate planning.

Tackling their retirement planning, the Doubletons
took a hard look into the future to see where they would be
in fulfilling their other long-term goals—buying a house
and educating their children—when the time for retirement
arrived. They assumed they would have achieved the first
goal in seven years; they further calculated that in 25 years
both children would have completed their education and
would be self-supporting.

"It means that in 25 years we can begin allocating
our long-term savings toward retirement," Jim figured.
"We'll have 15 years to build up a retirement fund."

Since Jim would then be 50 years old, he would be
saving for retirement during what should be his peak income years. His future earnings were hard to estimate,
but Jim decided that he might by that time hold the job
his boss now had.

"He's making about $20,000 now—so maybe I'll
make $30,000 if the rate of inflation continues. But let's
say I'll earn about $25,000."

Further calculations showed that if they were to set
aside 13 percent (their present long-term savings rate) of
Jim's expected salary during the 15 years leading to his
retirement at age 65, they would save between $55,000
and $60,000. They decided not to count on any extra in-
come in case Julia went back to work. But the interest on
their savings would give them about $2,900 of annual
retirement income. There would be additional income from
Jim's pension and from Social Security. To sum up, the
Doubletons' planned annual income during their retirement
years would look like this:

61

SOURCE	ANNUAL INCOME
Long-term savings account	$ 2,900
Social Security (estimated)	2,900
Pension income	8,000
Total annual retirement income	$13,800

In addition, the Doubletons realized that they might sell their house around retirement time. If they did sell, they planned to deposit their equity in a savings bank account where it would produce still more retirement income.

Be wise in time

Will things work out for the Doubletons precisely as planned?

No one can be absolutely sure, of course. But the odds are that they stand a far better chance than the non-planners of being among the "2 percent self-supporting" people after 65.

Many families include retirement provisions in their financial planning but underestimate their total income needs during retirement. They don't realize that life expectancy is a moving target. Some new actuarial tables show that of all men aged 35 today, almost two-thirds will be alive at age 65, and these can expect to live from 10 to 15 years longer.

So you might as well assume you're going to live to be at least 80 and plan for your retirement accordingly.

Many people today can count on retirement income from both Social Security and company pension plans. Even self-employed individuals—doctors, lawyers, small businessmen, farmers and others—as the result of federal legislation can now get an income tax deduction for money they set aside for retirement. Mutual savings banks in a number of states have the authority to offer this retirement plan service for people who are self-employed. The fastest way to learn more about such a tax-benefit retirement program is to ask your local savings banker if his institution has the power to provide this service.

From age 65 onward, you can expect your annual income to decrease by at least one third. Pension checks, Social Security benefits and income from your savings and investments will not compensate fully for the absence of regular paychecks, but many of your family expenses will be reduced.

Your life insurance policy will probably be paid up; if not, with your children no longer dependent, you can reduce your policy if you wish, to effect a saving in premium cost. The cost of educating your children will also be behind you. Routine expenses for food and clothing can be expected to go down, as will outlays for commuting and entertainment.

The income tax bite will be less painful since people over 65 currently can claim a double $600 exemption. If both husband and wife are over 65 and file a joint return, they can immediately establish an exemption base of $2,400. Since the exemptions and other deductions will be subtracted from less total income, your savings on taxes after 65 will be considerable.

Some costs go up

But don't expect to save much on medical expenses. Medicare and Medicaid, for which you become eligible at 65, will cover some—but not all—of the increased medical expenses that will be heading your way. Your medical bills will probably be from two to three times higher than when you were in your prime, so make sure you carry enough health insurance to make up the difference.

If you have not sold your house by the time retirement age arrives, you will at least want to start thinking of the possibility. Granted there will be many sentimental

63

attachments to this home and its special role in your family life. But the mere physical demands of keeping up a house can become a burden in the years of retirement.

Furthermore, the sale of your house could do two things for you financially during your retirement years. First, selling will unlock your equity, thus substantially increasing your liquid or cash assets; these can be deposited in a savings bank to increase your retirement income. Secondly, the sale will mean a big saving in home maintenance costs and in real estate taxes. However, this saving probably will be largely offset by the cost of your retirement housing.

Perhaps just as important is the new perspective and the new interests you will gain from moving out of the past and into the future. Remember: you have a considerable stretch of life ahead of you. A treasure house full of happy memories can be a great emotional asset as you adjust to a new way of life, but it may make equally good sense to convert the house itself into a financial asset.

A good solution may be to move into an apartment, and perhaps to a warmer climate after you dispose of the old homestead. In smaller quarters you will need less furniture. Before you move any of the excess furniture out of the house, talk to your real estate broker. These experts unanimously agree that you can sell a "full" house much more easily—and for a higher price—than one that is half full or shows wall-to-wall emptiness.

Cooperative or condominium?

If you sell your house (and of course you will be wise to select your new residence well in advance of the actual closing), and you want to return to apartment living instead of renting, as you probably did in your early married years, you may want to consider having your cake and eating it, too: investing in a cooperative or condominium apartment.

Most states have cooperative apartment laws, but condominiums are a relatively new way of investing in residential real estate, and they are becoming increasingly popular in some areas.

The main difference between a cooperative and a condominium is the way in which you establish ownership of the apartment. In the case of a cooperative, you don't actually own your apartment, but you do own shares in a nonprofit corporation that is the proprietor of the building. What you get for your money is the rights of a shareholder, and a proprietary lease. You pay a share of the building maintenance, operating costs, taxes and the corporation's mortgage and insurance expenses. You also maintain and decorate your co-op apartment.

Bear in mind, though, that co-op apartment carrying charges are not necessarily fixed. They can go up or down, depending on how the building is maintained, and on costs. Living in a cooperative apartment is *not* inexpensive. However, the part of your payment applied to mortgage interest and taxes on the building is tax-deductible.

If you want to move out of a cooperative, you must find someone to buy your shares in the proprietary corporation. Sometimes this proves hard, and you may end up selling your shares back to the corporation. But if you exercise reasonable care before you invest in a cooperative, the chances are you won't have too much trouble selling. There's an expanding market for cooperatives in many areas.

When you invest in a condominium, you buy in effect a chunk of the building—your apartment. You actually *own* your apartment and you pay taxes on it directly, as an individual, just as you did on your house. You have an individual mortgage. But don't expect to get as high a mortgage on a condominium as you might have had on your house: a two-thirds-of-value mortgage is about the maximum.

You also join with your fellow owners in a condominium building as the proprietor of its jointly used premises —halls, steps, parking area, etc.—and the same holds true for paying the costs of their upkeep and repair.

The tax advantages in owning a condominium are similar to those for a cooperative, but the chief advantage of condominium ownership is that you actually *own* the apartment itself. You may find it easier to sell the "brick-and-mortar" of an apartment than shares in a co-op, and you will have the benefit of any appreciation in its market value. Again, the selling price will largely depend on the demand for condominium apartments in your community, the location and amenities of the building itself and on the monthly operating costs, all of which you should have considered carefully before you bought the condominium in the first place.

Finally, a cooperative or a condominium apartment becomes part of your estate, so don't forget to include it in your estate planning.

Estate planning

A wise old lawyer once said, "We're all standing in one long line, of course, pointing in the same direction. The great enigma is your place in the line and when you will get to the head. Your place will be much more comfortable if you've planned your estate as though your turn will come tomorrow."

Lawyers know that in this age of huge inheritance taxes and of complex and extended probate the person who does his own estate planning, or who does none at all, has a fool for a client. A qualified attorney will more than earn his fee in helping you draw up your estate plan and to keep it updated. If you die intestate—without leaving a will—the state takes over, which may cause needless problems for your survivors.

As an example of the value of a will, consider what would happen if husband and wife should die simultaneously in an automobile accident. Without a will, the intestate settlement may result in a distribution that is entirely undesirable. If the husband and wife each have a will, each can specify the distribution of his and/or her estate in case of simultaneous death.

The time for estate planning arrives when you become legally competent to own property—in most states this is at the age of 21. Certainly you should have an estate plan when you get married; if both you and your fiancée have had the good sense to draw up your wills before your marriage, you'll no doubt want to change them after you get married.

Your attorney will not only draw up new wills with your family in mind, but he can also advise you on the appointment of an executor and co-executor.

The executor's chief function is to settle the estate of the deceased. The co-executor serves two useful purposes: he or she takes over the disposition of your estate if the executor should die or become legally incompetent. If you have named a law firm or bank as co-executor, it will handle such complicated problems as probating the will, paying estate taxes, meeting claims, liquidating or reinvesting assets as well as preparing for, and filing a final accounting with, the court.

One job you should handle yourself is the preparation of a letter of last instructions. This should be given to your executor and co-executor, to be opened after your death. It should include information covering your funeral and burial, the place where you keep your will and other valuable papers, and a list of your assets and liabilities. If you keep your valuable papers in a safe deposit box, make sure your letter of instructions indicates where the box is and where the key to it may be found.

A final word: planning your estate is not the most cheerful part of your financial responsibilities. But don't put it off; it should become an integral part of family planning early in a marriage.

HOW TO "NEST-EGG" $50,000 FOR RETIREMENT FUN

It seems like only yesterday! But it actually happened 15 or 20 years ago . . . . Only yesterday, your first baby was born. Today she's choosing her college or talking about marrying "the boy." Time flies. You realize it when you look backward. It is much harder to realize how time flies when you try to look ahead. Think about what you'll do when it's time to retire—in 20 years? Fifteen years?

If you ever hope to do a lot of things you've passed by in these last 15 or 20 years, you'll need **money.** Suppose you are 50 years old now and the youngsters' college expenses are behind you. But your peak earning years are now. If you put $200 a month—that's less than $50 a week—into a mutual savings bank account, you will have saved $36,000 in 15 years. And all during that time your mutual savings bank will have been adding a big interest dividend. You'll have a savings "nest egg" well over $50,000. You'll be 65. Time to enjoy life—do your own thing. Oh yes, and the grandchildren are coming for the summer . . . .

Chapter Seven

Buying a House

The biggest single purchase any family is likely to make will be a house, and the cost of houses is continually rising. For example, in April 1965 the average purchase price of already existing one-family homes was not quite $20,000. Three years later it had gone up to more than $23,000. While inflation is certainly one cause, other factors have also helped to push home prices up—among them increased land values and the demands of home buyers for more expensive features and more space.

These trends are likely to continue. They mean that the investment you make in a home today in all likelihood will appreciate in value by the time you decide to sell the house. This likelihood is especially important because the average American family no longer spends a lifetime in a single home. Today, family mobility is so great that many of us will live in half a dozen homes, or more, in a lifetime.

The time to buy

It is obvious that the average newly married young

couple, no matter how fond their dream of home owner-ship, will hardly be in a position immediately to afford the sizable outlay that will be needed to cover the down pay-ment on a house and the cost of furnishing it. But financial considerations are not the only reasons for holding off for a while.

A marriage brings together two individuals with sepa-rate—often different—backgrounds and living patterns. You have to find a common meeting ground, a common household and financial pattern. Renting will give you the freedom for trial-and-error learning about each other's needs and of household management during the early years of your new life together.

As we saw in Chapter Four, the Doubletons estab-lished a target period for buying their home—in seven years. These years allowed them time to save the cash they would need for home-buying. This period of saving is also an excellent time for deciding the kind of house you will want, where you want it, and for pricing the market.

How to compromise

Home-buying, like other important decisions, usually requires some compromise between what you want and what you can actually afford. Before you start on a seri-ous search you should list and agree upon the basic features your house *must* have—the number of bedrooms and baths you will need to accommodate your family, and the other imperatives such as an efficient kitchen layout (and modern appliances), ample closet and storage space, and a good overall floor plan.

Then, in order of priority, list the additional features you both desire—proximity to schools, churches, transpor-tation and shopping, a quiet street with little traffic, a gar-age, perhaps a playroom, laundry room, a separate dining room and a study or den for books and the hi-fi.

You'll also want to agree on whether you prefer a new or existing house, on what you would prefer in exterior design—ranch type, colonial, split level, contemporary, etc.—and in materials—brick, frame or other types of construction.

It is likely that you won't be able to afford everything your family desires, in addition to what you genuinely need in a home, *but don't compromise on what you must have for something you would like to have.*

When you've decided how much house you need, the next step—a vital one—is to judge how much you can afford to pay for it. There are several basic considerations, and you will need precise figures for each:

purchase price

monthly payments, including local taxes and insurance

operating expenses

Purchase price

Money management experts agree that as a general guideline the cost of a home should not exceed two and one-half to three times the family breadwinner's annual take-home pay. If this take-home pay amounts to $10,000 a year, then a house in the $25,000 to $30,000 price range is what the experts say is generally the maximum amount the family can safely spend.

But this is only a general guideline, something to give you a benchmark in deciding your own family's home price. When you make this decision, try to look ahead into your own future. For example, if the breadwinner's job involves his transfer to various other cities, you would be wise to forget about what your family's housing needs might be five or ten years from now and to buy a house that suits your needs today.

On the other hand, if he is not likely to be transferred elsewhere, if his future can be expected to offer him a rising income and if your family can be expected to grow, then you might profit from buying the maximum house you can afford and even consider going beyond the general guidelines for home costs. But be cautious about this.

How long a mortgage?

How much cash?

As for the actual purchase, there are three important questions to which you will want precise answers: (1) How much cash will you need at home-buying time; (2) how big a down payment should you make; (3) how many years should you take to repay your mortgage loan?

Let us take up the cash requirements first. Depending upon the kind of home loan you arrange, the minimum down payment required of you could range from approximately $3,000 to $6,000 for a $30,000 house.

In addition to your down payment, you should have sufficient cash to cover the usual "closing costs" such as appraisal and legal fees, title insurance, recording fee, mortgage tax, an advance payment of real estate taxes and advance insurance premiums. These additional initial costs vary in different areas, but they can easily add up to several hundred dollars. To prepare adequately, it is a good idea to check the level of such costs in your community well in advance of your decision to buy.

As for the size of the down payment and the term of your mortgage: should you make the absolute minimum down payment, or is it wise to put more money down if you can? And should your mortgage term be for 20, 25 or 30 years?

The amount of your down payment naturally will be determined in good part by how much savings you have available. But without question, the more you can afford to put down, and the fewer the years you need to repay your loan, the more money you will save in interest.

For example, some lending institutions adjust their mortgage interest rates according to the risk that is involved, so that you pay a lower rate of interest in return for making a substantial down payment. Whatever the interest rate, a larger down payment will significantly reduce the size of the loan and therefore the total interest charges you will pay over its life, as well as the size of your *monthly* payment.

The table below will give a clear-cut idea of the savings you can achieve with a more modest, shorter-term home loan.

TOTAL INTEREST CHARGES

on an amortized home loan of

No. of Years at	6½%	6¾%	7%	7½%
$15,000				
20	$11,841	$12,374	$12,912	$14,001
25	15,387	16,092	16,806	18,255
30	19,135	20,024	20,928	22,760
$20,000				
20	$15,788	$16,499	$17,214	$18,668
25	20,515	21,457	22,408	24,340
30	25,511	26,699	27,905	30,346
$25,000				
20	$19,736	$20,624	$21,519	$23,336
25	25,643	26,819	28,010	30,425
30	31,887	33,374	34,878	37,931

Carrying costs—how much can you manage?

These will cover your monthly payments of principal and interest on your mortgage balance, and often one-twelfth of your estimated annual real estate taxes and insurance.

Money management experts advise that a family's

monthly mortgage payment should not be more than one-fourth of the breadwinner's monthly take-home pay. Thus, if the breadwinner's weekly take-home pay is $160, the total of his family's monthly mortgage payment—principal, interest, real estate tax and insurance escrow—should not exceed that amount. But, again, this is merely a guide.

Every family presents a different set of budgeting requirements. A large family with many children would probably have to allocate less take-home pay for the monthly home mortgage payment than would a family with just one or two children.

Consider the operating expenses

Over and above your mortgage payment, you can figure on spending annually from 1 to 2 percent of your home's purchase price for its upkeep and maintenance, not including utility expenses. It pays to be alert to—and plan for—higher than normal expenses in this area that come right after the purchase of a home.

If it is your family's first home, you'll find the outlay rather heavy for such things as lawn furniture and equipment—a lawn mower, hose and the tools necessary for maintaining your property. And whether you are a first-time homeowner or not, usually the move into a new house means you will soon be shopping for new furniture, rugs and other household items. Plan ahead and save in advance for these needs.

Some final advice about that big step toward home-buying:

The demand for homes in our country is evidence that home ownership can provide one of the happiest periods in a family's life together—if it is not a financial strain to meet the costs involved. The simple secret to happy homeowning family life is: *don't buy too much house.*

This doesn't mean you should buy too little house

either. It merely means that you should save enough before you buy a home so that you can make a down payment that will bring your monthly payments well within the one-week's-salary formula recommended by money management experts.

And don't make the mistake of counting on more than one income to help meet the monthly costs of home ownership. Even if the mother is working, it is best not to depend on her income to meet your monthly payments. Why? If she stops working for any reason, even temporarily, you've got problems. It is far better to figure that the extra income a mother brings home is a *cushion*. Then you will not run into financial risks if such income stops.

Let us assume that you know how much house you need, have decided how much you can pay for it, have saved up enough money and have reached the point in time when buying a house *now* makes the most sense. You're ready for the next three steps:

1. *Spread the word.* Don't hesitate to enlist a private corps of assistants in your search. Tell your friends, relatives and co-workers that you are looking for a house and even what kind of a house you want. In our highly mobile society, families are continually moving in and out, from community to community, and often the first announcement of a vacancy is by word of mouth.

Also, many large companies that transfer employees regularly have established their own real estate departments. If your firm is in this category, be sure to check out its listings.

2. *Do your homework and "shop."* Try to find out everything you can about what is being offered for sale, and at what kind of price. When you see a listing in your price bracket, don't hesitate to examine the house even though, for one reason or another, you don't intend to buy it. Shopping around will give you a better idea of what a "spacious living room" really looks like. Match every listing you see against your own needs and desires to de-

termine if your own price bracket is realistically within the market.

Here is an additional tip, since you may find yourself "shopping" more than you expect: start a card file. List and describe each house you inspect and that appeals to you. This way you won't forget or become confused about comparative details.

A card file can save you needless trips to reinspect houses you've already seen. The basic details you'll want to record are: address; exterior design or style; price; age; number of rooms, bedrooms, baths; garage and basement size; type of heat; your impression of the neighborhood and the surrounding houses.

3. *Consult real estate brokers.* Helping families to buy and sell houses is their business, and they can save you a lot of time and trouble in locating the kind of house you want, especially if you are looking for an existing rather than a brand-new house. When you select a broker, it is a good idea to choose someone who is a member of the National Association of Real Estate Boards. He'll have a "NAREB Member" sign on display, and you'll know he is knowledgeable about the market.

Once you are at the point of *serious* house hunting, there are many more things you should check thoroughly. Here is a suggested checklist to follow if you're looking for an existing house, although many of these suggestions will apply equally well if you confine your house hunt to new constructions.

Outside the house

First, consider the location. Experienced real estate appraisers, when asked to name the three factors that most strongly influence a home's value, like to reply: "Location, Location, Location!" They are probably right. Is it reasonably close to schools, churches, playgrounds, public transportation and shopping facilities? What about fire and police protection? And what is the sewer and water situation?

Next, take a close look at the neighborhood. Are the other homes nearby well kept and in the same price range as the one you are looking at? It is generally best—in terms of long-term values—if all homes in a given neighborhood are in the same price range. Professional real estate appraisers have this theory on the neighborhood's influence on house prices:

A home will tend to go up in value if other homes around it are more expensive. It will tend to go down in market value if other homes in the area are in a lower price range.

What else should you check about your prospective neighborhood? The neighbors, of course. Are they about the same age as your family? Do they have children? Do they maintain their homes well? Also, be sure to ask about real estate taxes. What is the tax level now? Is it likely to go up substantially in the near future because of a need for new schools or expanded facilities, or for some other reason? Are there any special assessments against the property you are interested in?

Inside the house

Is everything in the house in working order—light switches, bathroom and plumbing fixtures, heating system and appliances?

Do all the doors and windows open and shut smoothly?

Do the roofing and basic structure seem to be in sound condition?

Are the steps too steep for carrying babies up and down, or are there other serious inconveniences?

Is the garage or carport big enough to accommodate your car . . . and maybe bikes, scooters, toys and lawn and garden equipment?

Are landscaping and shrubbery needed?   77

Even when your prospective house passes your check-list test with flying colors, it never hurts to hire a real estate appraiser—one who specializes in *residential* properties—to examine the house and neighborhood and give you a written report about them. The cost of this appraisal will be money well spent, considering the size of your overall investment, especially if the house you are seriously interested in is an older home.

Finally, if you decide to buy it, a lawyer will be extremely important to you—from the moment the contract of sale is drawn up right on through the closing of your mortgage loan. Among his services will be to make certain that all important details about the purchase appear correctly in the contract and that the deed to your house —your certificate of ownership—is in good legal order. There are many other details that will require his expert counsel and attention.

Financing your house

Just as this house is likely to be the biggest purchase your family will make, the means of financing it may also be your family's biggest credit commitment. If you take care in searching for your house, you should take at least as much care to find a mortgage best suited to your family needs.

Home mortgages come in all sizes, shapes and descriptions, but the fundamentals are all the same: a modern mortgage is a long-term loan to you (the nominal owner of real estate property), amortized and interest-bearing. You post the house with the lending institution—usually a savings bank, savings and loan association or commercial bank—as collateral until the loan is paid off. You, the borrower, become known as the mortgagor.

You agree to repay the lender, called the mortgagee, the amount you borrowed plus interest in regular monthly payments of a specified amount, over the term of the mortgage (usually from 15 to 30 years). You also are committed to carry adequate hazard insurance, to pay all property taxes and to maintain your property in good order.

One word about fire insurance. Replacement costs are on the rise, so don't hesitate to keep your home's fire insurance on the high side of estimates for what it would cost you to rebuild it from the foundation up.

In some areas it is common practice for institutions that give mortgages to ask for monthly payments to include, in addition to principal and interest, one-twelfth of the estimated annual cost for insurance and taxes. The lending institution puts these funds into a special escrow account until it is time to pay for the insurance and taxes in your behalf.

There are three basic types of home mortgages you should know about—FHA (Federal Housing Administration), VA (Veterans Administration) or GI, and conventional.

The FHA loan. Although insured by the Federal Housing Administration, this is made by private lending institutions according to standards and requirements established by the FHA. The FHA insurance protects the lender against loss should the home buyer default on his loan payments. The borrower, of course, must pay for this insurance—½ of 1 percent per annum of his mortgage balance. This ½ of 1 percent insurance premium is added to the federally established interest rate and is paid as part of the borrower's monthly mortgage payment.

On one-family homes, FHA loans up to $30,000 are available, with repayment terms ranging up to 30 years. The minimum down payment required on a $30,000 FHA loan is $3,700; however, as was pointed out earlier in this chapter, the family that can make a larger down payment will save considerable money.

The VA mortgage. This is available to veterans who have had more than six months of active service in the armed forces since the Korean war began. Like FHA loans, VA mortgages are given by private lending institutions according to government standards and requirements. The VA guarantee can cover up to 60 percent of a home mortgage, but $12,500 has been set as the maximum dollar amount of VA protection that is provided to the lender. The interest rate on VA home loans is established by the Veterans Administration to match the rate that is charged for FHA loans. However, there is no insurance premium charged for VA loans.

The objective of the federal government in both FHA and VA loan programs has been to share part of the loan risk with the private lender, thus enabling the private lending institutions to offer more liberal terms with smaller down payments than would be possible if the lenders assumed all the risk themselves. By making lower down payments, lower monthly mortgage payments and longer loan terms possible, these programs have brought home ownership within the reach of many millions of American families who might not otherwise have been able to afford a home of their own.

The conventional mortgage. The third common type of home loan is the "conventional" mortgage, made without federal government backing by private lending institutions, entirely at their own risk. Because under conventional mortgages they are shouldering the whole long-term risk, the lending institutions require a somewhat larger down payment, and the terms of the loan are somewhat shorter than for loans under FHA and VA programs.

For the past few years, the average *term* for conventional loans made by mutual savings banks, savings and loan associations, mortgage companies, commercial banks and life insurance companies has ranged from 24.7 to 25.2 years on new homes; it has averaged from 21.8 to 22.5 years on already existing homes. The *amount* of conventional loans has averaged about 73.5 percent of the appraised value of new homes and about 72.3 percent of the appraised value of already existing ones.

Some conventional loans are made under a package agreement whereby the mortgage covers not only the land and the house but also the major household appliances. Other loans may include an open-end feature that permits you to reborrow in order to make home improvements.

Where to find home financing

Most of the nation's home mortgages are made available by mutual savings banks and by savings and loan associations. Also, mortgage banking firms throughout the country are prominent as home mortgage originators. Commercial banks and insurance companies also make home loans, but these are not a consistent source of funds.

To see how dependent our nation is upon savings institutions for a steady flow of home loan funds, consider this fact: *approximately 75 percent of the savings bank industry's assets are invested in mortgage loans.* The savings banks and savings and loan associations combined hold about 60 percent of the outstanding home mortgage debt in this country.

A further indication of the extent to which mutual savings banks have involved themselves in helping to achieve the nation's housing goals has been their long record of lending in our so-called "inner cities." These activities cover mortgages to finance housing redevelopment for low-income families and loans to help inner-city residents buy, or to modernize houses.

Wherever you buy a house, its value will go up as the value of homes about you go up. Thus a family that plans to buy a house at some future date and is now saving toward that end should accumulate its savings where they will do the most good for all homes—in a family-oriented thrift institution such as a mutual savings bank.   81

HOW YOUR REGULAR SAVINGS GROW

(Calculated at 4½% interest; compounded quarterly)

How Much You Will Have on Deposit at the End of ...

Save This Much Weekly	1 Year	2 Years	5 Years	10 Years	20 Years
$ 5	$ 266.05	$ 544.28	$1,457.72	$ 3,280.97	$ 8,413.65
$10	532.10	1,088.56	2,915.44	6,561.94	16,827.30
$15	798.15	1,632.84	4,373.17	9,842.92	25,240.95
$20	1,064.21	2,177.12	5,830.89	13,123.89	33,654.61
$25	1,330.26	2,721.40	7,288.02	16,404.86	42,068.26

Chapter Eight

Planning
A Life Insurance
Program

One of the first decisions a young married couple should make while drawing up its financial plan is how much of its monthly take-home income to allocate for life insurance.

Americans appreciate the need for life insurance better than any other people in the world. In this country insurance on the lives of more than 130 million policyholders has now reached the hard-to-believe sum of $1.18 trillion. The average amount of life insurance owned per family is well over $17,000.

And in Connecticut, Massachusetts and New York a unique form of low-cost insurance can be bought from most mutual savings banks. Called "Savings Bank Life Insurance," it is available right in the savings bank offices to people who either live or work in the three states. An indication of the popularity of this low-cost insurance and its widespread impact in Connecticut, Massachusetts and New York is this: Currently, close to $4 billion of Savings Bank Life Insurance in individual policies and group certificates—covering approximately 1.2 million people—is in force in just these three states.

In spite of these impressive statistics, the fact remains that many people buy insurance without adequate knowledge of the insuring company, the types of policies and benefits that are available—and that they are buying—and the precise costs involved.

Before you buy life insurance, check the soundness of the *insurer* and make certain the company meets all the standards set by your state government. You can obtain this information by writing to the insurance department of your state or to the state insurance commissioner's office.

Make sure also that the policy you are considering is not priced higher than other companies' policies offering the same benefits. Price variation does exist in the insurance field, as in others. Since every family should anticipate that its investment in life insurance will be substantial over the years, even a small percentage of reduction in the cost of the premiums could add up to a considerable saving of dollars over the term of your policy.

At the same time, do not be lulled into thinking that the price of insurance is just a matter of the premium costs. It isn't.

How to judge costs

The premium cost in most cases is only the starting point. Many policies pay annual dividends back to the policyholders. These, of course, reduce the cost. Also, all policies other than term and group insurance have a *cash value*.

The traditional way to compare costs is to compare the 20-year net costs. This means taking the total of the premiums for 20 years, less any dividends that will be paid to you during that period, and also less the cash value at the end of the 20-year period. Most insurance company representatives can provide you with this figure; it will give you a rough approximation of the comparable costs of policies and insurers you are considering.

However, this calculation still gives you only a rough approximation of insurance policy costs because it ignores the *earning value* of your yearly premium payments. So whenever you compare the costs of similar types of insurance policies, issued by different insurers, the policies themselves must be read very closely to make certain that they offer the same benefits.

The role of insurance

With the exception of term insurance, all life insurance policies have two values:

1. Protection—the cash that will be paid to the beneficiary in the event of the death of the insured.

2. Savings—the cash that is guaranteed as payable to the insured person should he wish to discontinue the policy or borrow against it.

Endowment insurance, which provides for the payment of the policy amount if the policyholder is alive at the end of a specified period of time, as well as for payment in the event of his death prior to the endowment date, can also be considered a form of savings.

The two values of protection and savings are derived from the premiums that you pay. If you assume a given amount of premium, it is obvious that in any policy, if a larger portion of the premium is used to provide savings, a smaller portion is left to be used for protection. Therefore, the larger the savings element in any policy, the smaller will be the amount of protection per dollar of premium.

But while there may be both investment and savings elements in life insurance, always remember: its principal and unique function is protection. Protection should be the primary consideration for the young married couple in deciding how much insurance to carry and what kind is right for them.

When a young family expands with the arrival of children, its need for insurance protection will grow and will continue to increase to a point in time when the children are mature and the responsibilities of the parents begin to decrease. At this stage, the need for protection begins to lessen. The parents can then put more emphasis on making provision for a more generous retirement income in their insurance.

Since the role of insurance in family financial planning changes over the life cycle of the family, a young married couple should not lock themselves into a form of insurance coverage that is unsuitable to changing needs. How to make the right decision about insurance? You must first have some knowledge about the different kinds of coverage that are available.

There are scores of different kinds of policies, most of which are variations of three basic forms of life insurance: *term* coverage, *permanent or whole life* coverage and *endowment* insurance. Each of these three types has several variations.

How term insurance works

Term insurance gives you a specific amount of coverage over a specific time period—or "term." The face value of a term policy will be paid to your beneficiaries only if you die within the given period. Term insurance has the smallest premium payments of the three types because it provides only temporary protection. At the same time a given amount of premium dollars will buy more protection under term insurance than the same premium under any other type of policy.

Many term policies have a "conversion option." This allows the insured to switch to an equal amount of whole life or endowment insurance without undergoing another medical examination or furnishing the insurer with any other evidence of your insurability. When such a conversion is made, the premium costs increase. But the coverage period has been extended to cover the life of the insured, and furthermore cash values will now begin to accumulate.

Most term policies are renewable. That is, you can continue the same amount of coverage for a similar term (or for several such terms) without a second examination. In some policies, such a renewal is automatic; the insured does not need to notify the insurer that he wants his term coverage to be continued.

But again, the premiums when you renew will be higher, this time because you will be older. Since the risk of death increases with age, the cost of protection for your beneficiaries goes up accordingly.

The major characteristic of term insurance is that it contains *only* the element of protection without the element of savings. Because it is without a savings element, term insurance is sometimes called "pure" insurance.

Term insurance is available in forms that limit the period of coverage in different ways. For example, a policy may be for a term of five, ten or twenty years, or for a term extending to a specified age, such as 60, 65 or 70. The longer the term of a policy, the larger the premium will be.

Is decreasing term for you?

Some term policies give you the same *amount* of protection during the entire period, and others provide for a steadily *decreasing* amount of protection. A policy with a level amount of protection throughout its term will have a larger premium than one with decreasing coverage. The premium for decreasing coverage is the lowest of all policies available.

Policies with decreasing term coverage are practical when the need for the insurance declines. For example, this happens in the case of insurance to cover a reducing, or amortized, mortgage loan.

But when young families are determining their total insurance needs—present and future—they should not contract for decreasing term insurance as their only coverage. By doing so, they may lock themselves into a form of policy that is inflexible to any increasing needs.

Term policies with only limited conversion or renewal options, or with none at all, may carry a lower premium rate than policies that are more liberal. The lower rate might, in the long run, prove costly to you if later on you want to convert or renew. Thus the options have value, and they should be taken into consideration when you are analyzing any term insurance.

How to use group insurance

One form of very low-cost, renewable term insurance that has received wide acceptance in this country is group insurance. It is commonly available at one's place of employment or through an association of self-employed persons or some other form of organization such as a labor union, and you don't need a medical examination to be eligible.

Normally, this is term insurance without any cash or loan values. It provides protection only so long as you remain with the group; for example, only so long as the worker remains with the employer. Often the employer will pay all premium costs.

Group insurance should be regarded as additional rather than as a primary form of insurance coverage. Remember that group insurance is related to the job, and a change in jobs, even for a better job, may not always allow you the same, let alone a greater amount of protection. Even more important, however, is the fact that the amount of group coverage that is available seldom meets a family's total insurance needs.

Another form of term insurance is credit life insurance. This is provided through lenders of all types, and it insures the lives of borrowers at an amount that will be sufficient to repay the outstanding debt in the event of the borrower's death. By 1969 about $67 billion of such coverage was in force to protect more than 57 million persons.

Of all the various forms of term insurance, one of the most suitable for a young family's insurance protection needs is the five-year renewal-convertible term policy. This policy offers you a level amount of protection. Its premium rate is low at the beginning and so it allows you to buy a more substantial amount of protection.

Under it, every five years the protection renews, at a higher premium rate than during the previous five years (you are older), but the jump in the rate is quite small until the insured person reaches middle age. Also, the five-year renewable terms continue until the insured person reaches the age of 65 or 70. While other forms of term insurance may fit a particular set of circumstances, the flexibility of this policy makes it adaptable to most family needs.

The principal advantage of all forms of term insurance is the small payment needed to obtain substantial amounts of protection. Its main disadvantage is that the coverage is provided for only a specified period of time, and the buyer gets nothing back when the coverage period, or term, expires.

Insurance plus savings

Permanent or whole life insurance in its most popular form is called "straight life" or "ordinary life" insurance. It provides protection over the whole life of the insured. It combines the elements of savings and protection.

Straight or ordinary life policies require the smallest premium investment among the forms of permanent protection. They fit the needs of families who want to buy the highest amount of continuing protection for the smallest outlay in the payments that will recur over the life of the insured person.

Some people, realizing that the risk of death increases with age, find it hard to understand why the premium costs for simple whole life insurance remain the same over the many years of the duration of the policy. Here is the explanation:

The insurer establishes a "level" premium that actually is greater than the cost of the insurance during the early years of the policy, but less than the cost in later years. These excess payments of the early years, with accumulated interest, thus build up a "reserve" and this covers the higher cost of insurance as the person grows older. (In fact, it is this reserve that is the basis for determining the cash value that will be paid if the holder of the policy should turn it in before maturity.)

Insurers also have created a broad variety of what are called limited payment life policies that are designed to meet special needs. The "limited payment" life plan is a form of whole life insurance. It requires higher premium payments because all the premiums are payable within a specified time—usually in 15, 20 or 30 years, or at a specified age such as "life paid-up at 65." But although these premiums are higher than for the same amount of protection under a simple whole life policy, the cash and loan values are usually greater. This is a consideration to weigh when you make your choice.

Still, of the two types of whole life insurance— straight or limited payment—the straight kind is usually the better buy for a young family. Its lower premium investment is one reason. It also has flexibility. With each premium payment for straight life insurance, the policy builds up a higher guaranteed cash value. You can convert this at any time into a specified smaller amount of fully paid-up insurance. This option is guaranteed in most policies, it demonstrates the flexibility of whole life insurance.

Endowment insurance normally covers a given period of time—such as a 20-year endowment, or until the insured reaches the age of 65. If he should die before that time, his beneficiary will receive the face value of the policy. If he lives to the end of the period that was originally specified, the face value of the policy will be paid to him either in a lump sum or in installments.

Endowment insurance is distinctly a *savings* kind of policy. The premium payments are calculated to provide a cash value that is equal to the face amount of the policy at the end of the period stated. Obviously, the shorter the period, the larger the premium payments will have to be in order to build up the required amount of savings.

An endowment policy can be useful to an older person who has limited responsibilities and who wants to accumulate savings while carrying life coverage.

But for young people the endowment insurance plan has distinct disadvantages. It is the most expensive form of protection and thus it does not meet the young family's basic need—the greatest amount of protection at the lowest cost you can obtain. Another disadvantage is that, at the end of the endowment period, the insurance protection ends with the cash payment to the insured.

The endowment plan is also inflexible in that it may be difficult, if not impossible, to convert it into a lower premium form of whole life insurance. Generally the insurers will not permit such a conversion if the health of the insured person has become impaired or if he cannot meet certain requirements for whole life insurance coverage. In that case you would have to reduce the amount of the endowment policy or discontinue it altogether.

In summary, then, permanent insurance has these advantages over term coverage: it provides you with lifetime coverage, the premium doesn't change, and it builds savings against which you can borrow. Its principal disadvantage is the higher outlay required from you—usually at least twice as much for permanent as for term.

Explore combination plans

Many insurance companies—and Savings Bank Life Insurance in the three states where it is available directly from mutual savings banks—are now offering *combinations* of permanent and term insurance. These forms may be called "family income," "family maintenance" or "family provider" policies. They usually feature straight life insurance in varying amounts, level premium payments and either decreasing or level amounts of term insurance.

Their purpose is to guarantee a monthly income at a time when family responsibilities are greatest. The premium costs are relatively low and still assure a young married man that his wife and small children will have more adequate coverage than would otherwise be within their means if they were to buy only straight life insurance.

Another innovation—among the combination policies—is the blanket or package *family plan*. In this policy, a single contract usually provides permanent insurance for the father, a lesser amount of permanent coverage for the mother, and relatively small amounts of term coverage for the children. Generally, the policy will insure the mother up to the time her husband reaches retirement age, and it covers the children up to the age of 21 to 25.

Most family plan policies contain an option that allows you to convert the term insurance portion. This type of contract is ideal for the young family looking for the maximum protection at minimum cost.

Savings bank life insurance

A major boon for families living or working in Connecticut, Massachusetts and New York is Savings Bank Life Insurance (SBLI).

Like other savings bank services, SBLI was created in direct response to an urgent family need. It originated in Massachusetts in 1907 through the efforts of the late

Louis D. Brandeis, formerly justice of the United States Supreme Court, as a deliberate attempt to reduce the cost of one of the necessities of life. In his search for a form of insurance to replace the relatively high cost of industrial insurance with its weekly premiums, he conceived the idea of distributing life insurance through mutual savings banks.

Like many other public-spirited men, Brandeis was impressed by the history of the economic management of the mutual savings banks, their proven ability to invest funds safely, their local direction by trustees and by the high esteem in which they were held in their communities. Largely through his efforts, a savings bank life insurance bill was passed into law by the Massachusetts legislature in 1907.

For the next 31 years, Massachusetts was the only state in which SBLI was available. But in 1938 a bill sponsored by the late Governor Herbert Lehman won the approval of the New York State legislature. Three years later, at the urging of then Governor Robert A. Hurley, similar legislation was enacted in Connecticut.

Savings Bank Life Insurance has several distinct advantages:

1. *It is very low cost.* You must buy it directly from savings banks. By selling directly—over the counter or through the mail—the savings banks keep the insurance operating costs to a minimum.

2. *It has liberal cash values.* Savings Bank Life Insurance has cash and loan values that become available early in the life of the policy.

3. *It pays early dividends.* Life insurance sold by savings banks entitles the holders of policies to dividends, which banks pay as earned, starting at the end of the first year of premium payments.

4. *It has local, personal service.* In the three states that offer SBLI, families can receive impartial insurance advice and service at their local savings banks on any banking day of the year.

Separate state systems

In each of the three states where savings banks may offer SBLI, an individual insurance system functions with separate rules and regulations as directed by that state's laws. Currently, about 340 savings banks with a total of 885 offices in the three states offer Savings Bank Life Insurance as a customer service. The only limitation is that a person must live or work in the state—Connecticut, Massachusetts or New York—in which he purchases SBLI coverage. If a person moves to another state after he has bought SBLI coverage, his insurance *remains* in force.

The maximum amount of SBLI coverage a person can buy in the three states is determined by the insurance laws of each. While the laws dictate the specific policies that savings banks may sell over the counter, the banks offer in addition to the standard types of insurance policies—whole life, limited payment life, term and endowment—these forms of SBLI family protection:

Low-cost family package plan: Covers the mother, father and, up to a specified age, *all* children.

Family income term plan: Provides lump-sum payments and extra monthly income for the family in the event of death of the male parent during the children's critical "growing-up" years.

Home mortgage term: Low-cost decreasing term insurance with the cost reduced further through annual dividends paid to you as earned. Also has valuable conversion features.

Children's insurance: Available for children 15 days and up. No medical examination needed for children in good health.

Annuities: These guarantee you an income for life during your retirement years.

Group insurance: A range of low-cost plans for employers, government employees, members of charitable or religious associations and other groups.

Making your final choice

A young family's basic insurance need is protection. But most young married couples find themselves in a quandary when it comes to choosing the proper amount of life insurance, not realizing that at best their decision will have to be a compromise between what they need and what they can afford. The truth is that the average young husband with a growing family very frequently cannot afford all the protection he needs. His choice usually must center on the lower-cost premium plans with the most built-in protection he can get that is commensurate with his income.

But just how much protection does he need? This is the difficult question.

One rule of thumb tells us that insurance protection should be at least three times the annual income of the principal wage earner. In effect, it should be an emergency fund to tide the family over, without undue hardship, during the necessary and difficult period of adjustment that follows a tragedy in the family.

But while a three-times-annual-income policy may be adequate for some families, it may not be nearly enough for others. In fact, there are too many variables among families to generalize—the buyer's age, the number and age of the dependents, the family's standard of living, other insurance coverage, any debts that may be outstanding, the family's long-term goals and its savings plan and other considerations.

List your family's needs

Perhaps a better approach to the question of "Just how much insurance protection?" is to develop a list of your family's needs and to deduct from this the assets that you now have and that will be available to cover these needs. Here, for example, are some needs you might list: 95

1. Final expenses—burial, medical costs, etc.
2. Income for surviving spouse and children until the children can earn their own way.
3. Money to pay for mortgage or to cover rent payments.
4. Money to pay for education of the children.
5. Income for the surviving spouse—during the period after the children are grown—and in old age.
6. Emergency funds to cover unforeseen events.

When you compute your family assets, don't forget to include the income from Social Security benefits and any other insurance plans provided for you by your employer, as well as your savings and investments. Of course, you will want to include in the calculation of your assets any personal life insurance you already carry.

Social Security benefits to count on

Most people think about Social Security in terms of income during their retirement years. But that is not the whole story.

If you've worked long enough under Social Security —and most people have—you can count on having a continuing cash income for yourself and your family if you should become disabled. Also, your dependent survivors will receive monthly cash benefits if you should die. These benefits should be considered when you figure out how much insurance you need.

A person is fully covered under Social Security if he has credit for one quarter of a year of work (three months) for each year after 1950, up to the year he reaches retirement age or up to the year of his disability or death. In counting the years after 1950, anyone born in 1930 or later would not be eligible for those years before he reached age 22.

Even if a worker is not fully covered, certain kinds of Social Security benefits may be paid to his survivors if he is "currently" covered when he dies. He is currently covered if he has credit for at least one and one-half years of work within three years before his death. This would qualify him for monthly cash benefits to his children and their mother while she has them in her care.

The amount of the monthly retirement or disability payment is based on your average earnings under Social Security over a period of years. Payments to your dependents or survivors in case of your death also depend on the amount of your average earnings.

The table on page 98 illustrates what your Social Security benefits would be under a variety of circumstances, as of the date this book was published.

To summarize, the amount of life insurance coverage must always be made in the context of the family's total financial plan, except that now the protection of the family in the event of death is the main consideration.

The family that regards life insurance as merely a fund for paying burial and other expenses resulting from a death inevitably winds up underinsured, since the amount of protection should also cover, at least in part, the major needs of the survivors—among them, for example, educational costs for the children.

On the other hand, when families mistake life insurance for a substitute for savings or investments, they inevitably will be "buying" savings or investments on a high-cost basis.

There is an optimum amount of life insurance—neither too much nor too little—for every family. And each family must determine this particular amount for itself. Basically, each family must answer these two questions:

1. What are its present and future insurance requirements?

2. Which type of coverage will meet these needs at the lowest possible cost?

Each family should be aware that its insurance needs   97

Examples of Monthly Social Security Cash Payments

Average yearly earnings after 1950 [1]	$899 or less	$1800	$3000	$4200	$5400	$6600	$7800
Retired worker — 65 or older Disabled worker — under 65	55.00	88.40	115.00	140.40	165.00	189.90	218.00
Wife 65 or older	27.50	44.20	57.50	70.20	82.50	95.00	105.00
Retired worker at 62	44.00	70.80	92.00	112.40	132.00	152.00	174.40
Wife at 62, no child	20.70	33.20	43.20	52.70	61.90	71.30	78.80
Widow at 62 or older	55.00	73.00	94.90	115.90	136.20	156.70	179.90
Widow at 60, no child	47.70	63.30	82.30	100.50	118.10	135.90	156.00
Disabled widow at 50, no child	33.40	44.30	57.60	70.30	82.70	95.10	109.20
Wife under 65 and one child	27.50	44.20	87.40	140.40	165.00	190.00	214.00
Widow under 62 and one child	82.50	132.60	172.60	210.60	247.60	285.00	327.00
Widow under 62 and two children	82.50	132.60	202.40	280.80	354.40	395.60	434.40
One child of retired or disabled worker	27.50	44.20	57.50	70.20	82.50	95.00	109.00
One surviving child	55.00	66.30	86.30	105.30	123.80	142.50	163.50
Maximum family payment	82.50	132.60	202.40	280.80	354.40	395.60	434.40

[1] Generally, average earnings are figured over the period from 1950 until the worker reaches retirement age becomes disabled or dies. Up to 5 years of low earnings can be excluded. The maximum earnings creditable for social security are $3,600 for 1951-1954; $4,200 for 1955-1958; $4,800 for 1959-1965; and $6,600 for 1966-1967. The maximum creditable in 1968 and after is $7,800, but average earnings cannot reach this amount until later. Because of this, the benefits shown in the last two columns on the right generally will not be payable until later. When a person is entitled to more than one benefit, the amount actually payable is limited to the larger of the benefits.

Editor's note: Under Social Security, a widow with no dependent children is not eligible for widow's benefits until she is 60 years of age.

Widow under 62 and two children	82.50	132.60	202.40	280.80	354.40	395.60	434.40

Editor's note: Under Social Security, a widow with no dependent children is not eligible for widow's benefits until she is 60 years of age.

will change as the life cycle of the family changes over the years. It is not enough simply to buy life insurance; the challenge is to buy the right kind of insurance and the right amount commensurate with the family's long-term goals. The essential consideration in buying life insurance is to choose the proper policy to fit your family's particular needs.

Figure the lost-earnings factor

One of the mysteries surrounding insurance is the long-term net cost of a policy to the buyer. The *annual net cost* is a simple matter to determine, as we saw early in this chapter.

The going gets sticky, however, when we attempt to compute the *real long-term costs*. Some people believe that all they have to do is add up the cost of the annual premiums, over 20 years, then deduct their expected dividends and the surrender value of the policy, and the answer will be the policy's 20-year net cost.

But it isn't that simple.

How about the *earning value* of those yearly premium payments? For example, suppose the same amount of money had been put into a savings bank account? In other words, there is a "lost-earnings" factor that should also be taken into consideration in figuring the true long-term cost of insurance.

Those insurance "extras"

Most insurance policies can be expanded from the basic protection that has been discussed to provide extra coverage in the form of riders. These provisions beyond the basic contract will produce extra benefits or options for the policyholder. The more common of these riders cover insurability protection, family income, disability waiver and double indemnity. Here is what each means: 99

Insurability protection. The young married man will find this type of coverage worth exploring. Essentially, it gives the insured party the right to buy extra insurance in specified amounts as he grows older (usually there is a cutoff year at age 40) without any additional medical examination. The option continues even if the insured person becomes disabled or ill. The cost of this rider, which in effect guarantees your insurability, is low.

Family income. Under this rider, the insurer pays the family an income every month—over a specified period— should the insured die within a certain time. At the end of the specified period, the insurance company pays the face amount of the straight life policy, either in a lump sum or on a schedule that has been agreed upon. This type of rider actually is a form of decreasing term insurance; its advantage is that the premiums are lower than for a separate policy offering equal protection.

Disability waiver. One of the more useful forms of riders is this extra coverage, which for a small additional premium enables your policy to continue in force even though you yourself may become disabled. There is usually a cutoff age, at 60 or 65. Should you become disabled for at least six months, the insurer pays all premiums for you, beginning with the time when the disability began. All the provisions of the original contract remain in effect, including the building up of cash value and your right to borrow against it.

Double indemnity. This rider guarantees the payment of double (and in some cases triple) the face value of the policy if the insured dies in an accident. It is important to check thoroughly the policy provisions defining the conditions under which both disability waiver and double indemnity benefits are paid.

How will the insurer pay?

The most common form of life insurance settlement is the lump-sum payment—or "payout"—whereby the beneficiary gets the whole face value of the policy at once. But there are several other forms of settlement that Savings Bank Life Insurance contracts offer in common with other insurers.

Life income option. In one sense, this option makes a policy a form of annuity since SBLI agrees that in the event of the death of the insured, it will pay certain sums periodically during the life of the beneficiary. The amount of these payments varies in accordance with several factors, including the life expectancy of the beneficiary and, of course the face value of the policy.

Interest option. This form of settlement specifies that the face value of the policy will be left on deposit with SBLI and that SBLI will pay interest on it to the beneficiary while it has the use of the proceeds. This option is often used when the beneficiary is a minor. Usually it is accompanied by a clause in the contract that frees the proceeds for withdrawal when the minor comes of age. In some cases, provision can be made for withdrawal in the event of emergencies.

Fixed amount option. The proceeds of the policy are paid to the beneficiary periodically, in fixed amounts, until they are consumed.

Fixed period option. Under this option, there is a payout schedule specifying a number of years during which the beneficiary receives the proceeds. They are paid in equal installments.

It should be clear by now that life insurance is an essential form of protection that ought to be an integral part of every family's financial plan. But it is not the be-all and end-all of successful financial planning.

A balanced family financial plan will focus *first* on adequate savings, as did Julia and Jim Doubleton, with insurance coverage next on the priority list.

A FEW CAUTIONS ABOUT INSURANCE

Above all, don't take your insurance policy for granted.

These are some of the questions your policy should answer:

How often can you make payments, and is there a discount when you make annual or semiannual lump-sum cash payments?

Is there a grace period allowed to you after payments fall due, before the policy is canceled? If so, for how long?

As you build up cash value of the policy, how much do you keep if the policy is canceled?

Do you have the choice of having dividend payments allocated for buying more insurance, increasing the cash value or lowering the premiums?

What are the provisions for naming beneficiaries? Can you choose more than one, and can you name contingent beneficiaries? If so, how many?

Chapter Nine

When and How to Invest in Stocks

Most people are familiar with the ancient biblical wisdom that everything has an appropriate season—"a time for sowing and a time for reaping." There is also a time for saving and a time for investing. For the average family, the time for saving comes well ahead of the time for investing, but once your savings program is in hand you'll want to consider when and how to invest.

You may recall that the first decision Jim and Julia Doubleton made after getting married was to accumulate $5,500 in a savings bank account as "liquid savings for unforeseeable needs or emergencies." Every family should have such a pool of liquid assets—cash or near cash that is immediately available when needed. But the amount of liquid savings will vary from one family to the next.

Therefore the question of how much to keep in an emergency savings fund must be answered within the framework of each family's financial plan. Many financial counselors advise that a minimum savings fund should equal one year's income. The family that follows the Doubletons' example of a 25-percent-of-income savings program will have no problem accumulating enough savings to cover emergencies.

Actually, a regular family program of deposits in a mutual savings bank is not only a wise practice that guarantees the security and availability of your cash reserves; it also is an excellent investment—with built-in inflation protection. For example, a $10,000 deposit in a savings bank paying 5 percent interest compounded quarterly will grow to $16,436 in 10 years, to $21,072 in 15 years, and to $27,015 in 20 years.

But in all likelihood as the family matures, as its net worth continues to grow, as its goals are achieved one by one, the time for investing will arrive. It can be a most rewarding time—or a time of disaster.

How to handle your investment program

Everyone wants to put money to work to make more money.

A rage to own securities has swept the nation. Before you invest be sure to investigate—it will pay off. First, consider these statistics:

There are about 24 million owners of stocks in the United States. Some 4 billion shares are traded annually with a dollar value of nearly $150 billion.

There are more than 4,000 registered brokers and dealers. Including the registered representatives of these firms, the total number of people selling stocks and bonds exceeds 150,000.

The total market value of stocks and bonds outstanding exceeds $1.3 trillion—well above the gross national product.

This is the world of securities in its broad dimensions—a great amorphous mass of people buying and selling a great amorphous mass of stocks and bonds. (Incidentally, many books on consumer finance at this point would devote several chapters to a description of the basic differences and distinctions among the many varieties of stocks and bonds, and would touch upon the function of the securities markets. But there is the real danger that such a condensed description does the reader a disservice rather than providing him with a reliable guide through the complexities of the world of securities.) The reader who contemplates handling his own investments should study several volumes on the subject, beginning with the primers put out by the New York Stock Exchange, avoiding, of course, all the highly publicized, often disastrous how-to-make-a-million schemes.

Three theories

There's nothing wrong with managing your own investments once you've done your homework and learned to distinguish between the facts and non-facts about investing. Many of these non-facts are theories which have been given so much currency that they have gained the stature of facts. These include:

(1) Although stock prices may go up *or* down over the short term, over the long run—as shown by the performance of the popular Dow-Jones Industrial Average—stock prices can be expected to go up.

Let's examine this theory in the light of the stock market's performance over the past 50 years. In 1919, the yearly high of the Dow-Jones Industrial Average was 118.92. But five years later it was down to 88.33. Then over the next five years it rose to 318.17, a point it reached in 1929. It then fell over the cliff, hitting the bottom in 1932 at 41.22.

In other words, in 1932, the DJIA was only one-third as high as it had been in 1919, 14 years earlier. Surely 14 years would be considered a "long run" by any standard.

From its 1932 bottom, the DJIA then began a long uphill struggle. It did not reach its 1919 level again until 1935. It did not reach the 1929 level until 1954—a quarter of a century after the Big Crash.

More recently, the DJIA passed a historic milestone, in February 1966, when it temporarily cracked the 1,000 barrier. But shortly thereafter it went down again. And almost three years later it was still trying to regain the 1,000 level. Where will it be tomorrow? Next month? Next year? Or ten years from now? The answer: *no one knows*. And that is a *fact*. What this points up is that while the Dow can be expected to go up over the long term, this is not consistently true.

(2) Another popular theory has it that the most sensible investment is to buy such recognized blue chips as General Motors and American Telephone on a continuing basis and salt these securities away as the foundation of your portfolio of stocks. Now let's suppose you entered the market in 1966 and bought shares of both. General Motors was then selling at 105 and American Telephone around 75. In the fall of 1968, however, General Motors was selling in the 80's and American Telephone in the 50's. On that foundation, your portfolio would seem to be going nowhere.

(3) Then there is the theory of dollar-averaging— you should buy a stock at regular specified intervals, once every month, for example—whether it goes up in price, remains unchanged or goes down in price. If you follow this procedure, you will reduce the average cost per share over the long term.

But how about the dollar-averagers who were buying Brunswick stock when it hit a peak at 78 in 1962? Did they keep dollar-averaging when it hit the skids all the way down to 8? How about those color TV stocks that were the craze in 1965? Motorola, for instance, went all the way up to 233. But then it went down to 98. What did the dollar-averager do?

Dollar-averaging can be a very expensive theory. And that's another *fact*.

For every theory in Wall Street there is a counter-theory. For every fact there are a hundred fictions. Buying a stock—any stock, no matter how reputable it may seem—is a risk. When you invest in stocks you not only are "buying a share of America," *you also are risking money you should be able to afford to lose—money whose loss will not wipe out your plans to gain financial independence.*

Does this mean that the odds weigh heavily against your success in the stock market? It depends on how you go about it. If you handle your own securities, you will be joining the millions of amateurs who manage their own investments. Wall Street, like golf, is divided into two classes of participants: the professionals and the amateurs. Less than 1 percent of the 24 million investors in the United States are the professionals—the people who make their living out of the stock market. These include some 4,100 officers and partners of investment banks and brokerage firms, about 3,000 mutual fund and other institutional managers and advisers, and about 11,000 security analysts.

These are the professionals, the insiders.

Everyone else is an outsider, an amateur. And this means *you.*

One of the basic axioms that insiders follow is to "sell on the news." Let's see how this works.

Recently, for example, some of the insiders have been studying the so-called "convenience" stocks. These are offered by the companies whose research is directed at turning out products to make the life of the housewife easier. Suppose one of these firms develops a method of packaging a highly palatable, deep-frozen complete meal, as ordered by any family. A housewife would be able to telephone a menu and delivery instructions for a whole week's meals. The impact of such a development is bound to be tremendous.

Security analysts have already completed their studies of such impact of pre-prepared meals, delivered to the home as ordered, on the many industries that would be affected. Now suppose that some insiders are already

107

beginning to accumulate a number of the more promising stocks, with the result that these will start to move up in price. Other insiders will follow suit (the insiders trade such information back and forth via their private grapevines, without a word being publicized).

As these stocks begin to move up, they inevitably attract the attention of the business and financial press. Meanwhile, market letters are being sent out by brokerage and research firms, calling attention to this new development. Now these stocks really begin to zoom; then the outsiders—the amateurs—rush in; the insiders "sell on the news"—and turn to something else, their pockets ajingle.

Remember that *every time someone sells a share of stock, there must be someone else to buy it.* The insiders make a very comfortable living (and many make large fortunes) out of the stock market because so many millions of amateurs go it alone—and buy what the professionals sell.

Admittedly there are amateurs who now and then make a killing in the stock market. Some of them are just lucky; some of them have an insider as a close friend or relative. But on the whole, the average amateur has about as much chance of beating the stock market professionals as the average golfing amateur has of winning on the professional golf circuit.

"Well, how should I run my investment program?" you ask. "I want to invest to make a profit—but with minimal risk!"

The answer by now ought to be clear: pay a professional to run it for you. For example, pick a good mutual fund, then channel your investments into it, according to your financial plan. Forget about that dream of making a killing in the stock market.

Choosing a "good mutual fund" is not as easy as it may seem. There are some 400 mutual funds—they are good, bad and indifferent. Before you select one you should first know how a mutual fund works.

All mutual funds are *investment pools*. A mutual fund collects its pool of investment funds by selling its own shares. Then it acquires a portfolio of securities that show promise of increasing in value. Contrary to what seems to be a popular misconception, if you buy into a mutual fund, you do not become a fractional owner of each of the stocks in the fund's portfolio. You become a shareowner of the fund.

It is the same as buying an ownership interest in the market value of a basket of eggs. The man who manages the basket decides which eggs to buy and sell. You have no role in the decision-making process. If you want to sell your ownership interest, the man with the basket will buy it back from you at a price that reflects the total market value of all the eggs in the basket, divided by the number of shares you own.

Thus the price of a mutual fund's shares is the precise market value of its total assets divided by the number of shares in the fund that have been sold. You can buy mutual fund shares either directly from the fund through fund salesmen or sales agencies, or through one of a number of brokerage houses that may be selling the shares on a commission basis.

"Load" and "no load" funds

There are two basic types of mutual funds—"open-end" and "closed-end." Closed-end funds generally have a fixed number of shares that are traded on the stock exchanges or on the over-the-counter market.

More popular and familiar are the open-end funds which do not have a fixed number of shares and are purchased from the fund, its representatives, or through a brokerage house. To purchase shares of some open-end funds, you pay a sales commission or "load" charge; other such funds make no sales or load charge and are known as "no-load" funds. The operators of load and no-load funds traditionally collect a management fee. Such a fee is based on a percentage of the fund's assets, and it covers the cost of providing investment advice and doing the necessary bookkeeping—plus a profit for the management group. This management fee is deducted "off the top" of the fund's assets and thus reduces the value of each shareholder's ownership interest in the fund. At present, some regulatory authorities feel that both the sales commission charges and fees of the funds have been excessive, and federal legislation has been proposed that would force reductions. How successful this effort eventually will be remains to be seen.

In selecting a mutual fund, choose one with investment policies and practices that are in line with your own financial plans. Mutual funds generally buy and sell securities in keeping with their announced goals: growth or income or a balance of both.

A growth fund concentrates on stocks with the best potential for price appreciation. The amount of money paid out every year in dividends is a secondary consideration.

An income fund looks first for dividend or interest income.

A balanced fund, usually the most conservative kind, spreads its investment beyond common stocks to include preferred stocks and bonds.

There has been a great deal of recent publicity about the "go-go" or "performance" funds. Essentially, a go-go fund is one with an aggressive management that seeks stocks with the best price appreciation possibilities. These funds are different from other growth funds in that: (1) they invest in comparatively few stocks; (2) they have a turnover rate—the rate at which the fund's assets are bought and sold—considerably higher than the typical mutual fund industry rate of 20 percent or so; (3) they usually move up the fastest in a rising market—and fall the fastest when the market sells off. This means that you must remember this about the go-go funds: while they can be expected to go up faster, they also can be expected to go down faster.

What kind of mutual fund should your family buy?

This will have to be your decision, one based on a solid foundation of adequate family savings and life insurance protection. Remember, the function of mutual funds is to offer individuals, who can afford risk, an opportunity to pool investment dollars and, under the guidance of professional management, seek better investment results collectively than they could individually. Thus your ultimate objective should be to find a mutual fund that offers you suitable potential within the limits of your personal financial objectives. What procedure can you follow in selecting a mutual fund?

First, check a fund's prospectus for the statement it will contain on investment objectives and policies. Federal law requires every fund to state these policies clearly in a prospectus. You'll find mutual fund ads in newspapers and magazines suggesting that you write for a free prospectus.

Next, look into the fund's performance record.

Third, find out what charges, fees or costs are levied on the fund's investors. Is there a "load" charge involved when you buy shares in the fund? Is there a redemption charge when you redeem your fund shares? What are the fund's operating costs and what is the management fee charged by the fund's operators? And, finally, be certain that the fund's minimum share purchase requirements are not so large as to strain your family budget and endanger your overall financial plan.

Assuming reasonably comparable performance records, then on the cost side it would seem ideal if a fund makes no load or redemption charge and has low operating costs. You will want to search out the one fund that offers you the best "mix" of these cost advantages and your investment objectives.

STOCK VALUES—DO THEY ALWAYS GO UP?

Here is a clear picture of stock prices since the Great Depression of 1929-32. Popular mythology holds that over the long term stock values in general (as opposed to the fortunes of specific stocks) always rise. But notice that it actually took 25 years for the famous Dow-Jones average of industrial stock prices to climb back to its 1929 high point, after the low of 1932. How would this speed have affected your family financial plans?

Chapter Ten

Using Credit Wisely

Few would argue with this statement: "Economic growth in the United States has been stimulated to a great degree by the availability of mass financing and its sensible use." What this statement points up is these data: since 1950, consumer credit that is outstanding has grown from $21.4 billion to about $90 billion—a fivefold increase. Obviously installment credit buying answers a popular need. Most of us do buy on credit at one time or another. The trick is, however, to know how to use installment credit wisely. If you do you will be saving your family countless dollars.

The wise use of installment credit involves two specific points: (1) knowing when to use it and (2) knowing where to get it. The "Guide to Successful Family Living," which is based on reports of marriage counselors in the 335 voluntary agencies of the Family Service Association of America, has this to say about the use of installment credit: "Marriage counselors report an increasing number of married couples who overspend for 'instant gratification' —the satisfaction of all their desires for luxuries *at once,* 113 as if there were no tomorrow. . . . Other young couples need the ego-bolstering of owning expensive cameras, stereo phonographs, elaborate tape-recording setups, color television."

Continuing, the family service guide gives this warning about credit buying: "It is hard nowadays to accept our financial limitations, whatever range they may fall in. We are stimulated by advertising; and the availability of installment purchasing and easy credit makes it harder to resist buying than if cash-on-the-barrelhead were required."

What the family service guide suggests is moderation in the use of installment credit. In other words, know *when* to use it and know when *not* to use it. Above all, do not overload your family budget with installment loan debt.

The second important point in your installment credit know-how is the matter of finding these loans available on the most favorable terms, and where to look for them. The rate of interest charged for installment loans varies from community to community and from one type of lender to another. So always be sure to "shop" the lenders in your community thoroughly should you need an installment loan. This has been made easier by Truth-in-Lending laws enacted in some states and, most recently, by the federal government, which make it easy for borrowers to learn the dollar cost and the rate of true annual interest.

The major sources of consumer installment debt are banks, sales finance companies, retail outlets, credit unions and consumer finance companies. In many instances, the cost of this credit is more expensive than most borrowers realize.

Here are some examples of the true annual or effective rate of interest charged under various installment credit plans:

Unpaid balance plan. When you pay interest by the month on the unpaid balance of your loan, the effective or true annual rate of interest charged is 12 times the percentage that is quoted to you. If the rate quoted is 1½% per month on the unpaid loan balance, for example, the effective or true annual rate is 18%.

Opening balance loan. You pay interest by the month on the initial amount of your loan, and the true annual rate of interest charge will be close to double that of the unpaid balance loan described above. A monthly charge of 1½% on the initial amount of your loan produces a true annual interest rate of about 32%.

Discount loan. For each $100 that you borrow, a specified dollar amount is charged for every year over which you repay. The true annual rate of interest figures out to be about twice the specific amount quoted to you as discounted. For example, if the discount is $5 per $100 borrowed, the effective or true annual rate of interest will be 9.58%.

Let's say you wish to borrow $500 for one year and it is discounted at a rate of $5 per $100 per year. To get the $500 in cash you would sign a note for $526.32 and you would repay the latter amount in twelve payments of $43.86.

Discount loans are the common practice of savings banks and commercial banks when they make unsecured personal loans.

Add-on loan. A variation of the discount type loan is called the "add-on" loan. Here the effective or true annual rate of interest is just a shade less than for a comparable discount loan. For example, a one year add-on loan for $500 carrying a $5 per $100 charge would have an effective or true annual rate of 9.10% and you would pay back $525.00 in 12 equal monthly payments.

Generally speaking where savings banks offer these loans, the interest rate they charge will be the lowest in the community.

The true annual interest rate charged by the many other sources of unsecured installment credit varies widely. Here are some examples:

Small loan companies. Depending on what region of the   115 country they operate in, the true annual rates they charge range from 18% to 42%.

Retailers. Here the true annual rate is typically 18% to 20% and up.

Auto dealers and finance companies. Car loans from these sources typically carry a true annual interest rate of between 12% and 34%.

Department store revolving charge accounts. These usually carry an 18% true annual rate on unpaid balances up to about $500; on the portion of the balance above $500, the rate typically is 12%.

Department stores and other retailers. For expensive purchases such as appliances, these sources have installment credit plans. Usually the plans carry monthly interest rates charged on the loan's unpaid balance and these vary from 1½% to 3½%. They produce a true annual interest rate of between 18% and 42%.

The important point to bear in mind is that you don't merely use credit—you *buy* it. So if you find it necessary or expedient to undertake some buy-now-pay-later financing, make sure you shop around for your best credit buy.

Finding low-cost loans

"If you need money, really need it, don't be afraid to approach your relatives. They are the one group of lenders who can afford to take your word when the facts are against you. What's more, if you don't pay them back, it's all in the family. The money, in some cases, is considered by the lender to be an inheritance before-the-fact—when you need it most."

So advises Robert Metz in his book, *How to Shake the Money Tree.* Mr. Metz for years authored a column in *The New York Times* called "Personal Finance," and what he recommends is doubtless the lowest-cost loan of all—the homemade loan from Aunt Nelly or Uncle Mike.

116 But unfortunately for many millions of families who

use consumer credit at one time or another, not everyone has a well-to-do relative who can come through when credit is needed. The best advice for most families needing to borrow is *first to consider a collateral loan*—a loan that is secured by some form of asset such as a savings passbook or an insurance policy.

Loans against insurance policies have the double advantage of being relatively low-cost—5 to 6 percent—while offering a repayment schedule you can tailor to suit your own convenience. Actually, the insurance company won't nag you for repayment of the principal as long as you maintain the interest payments. Only permanent insurance policies (whole life, twenty payment life, endowment) can be borrowed against. Term policies, except in rare instances, have no such "cash" value.

An insurance policy loan does have two disadvantages: (1) it reduces the face value of the policy; (2) it can get expensive since repayment can be put off as long as the borrower wishes. So if you make an insurance loan, set yourself the earliest possible repayment schedule—and live up to it.

As we mentioned in another chapter, mutual savings banks offer two types of installment loans. In 11 states they may offer regular *unsecured*—or consumer—loans. And in all states most savings bank depositors can borrow against their savings accounts.

The rates charged by savings banks for regular consumer loans are almost always lower than those charged by other local sources. And in the passbook loan depositors have a truly economical, fast and painless collateral loan at their disposal.

In this instance the borrower merely posts or "pledges" his passbook as collateral and pays a minimum charge for the money he uses. Of course, the fundamental requirement for obtaining a passbook loan is that you have at least as much money in your savings account as you wish to borrow, for you cannot borrow more than you have in savings.

Many families have used their savings bank deposit accounts as a pool of borrowing funds for financing purchases of automobiles and home appliances or to satisfy other important needs for short-term or medium-term cash (i.e., one to three years). For example, if a family takes out a $3,000 passbook loan to buy a car, it can pay for the car in cash, thereby eliminating the need for higher-cost credit. Meanwhile, the $3,000 continues to earn interest while the book is pledged. If the savings bank's deposit interest rate is 5 percent, and the passbook borrowing rate is 6 percent, the out-of-pocket cost to the borrowing family is only 1 percent.

Still, always remember that a savings account exists to meet your true "must" needs before it serves your luxuries. Do not endanger funds set aside for genuine needs, or to meet unexpected emergencies, in order to borrow for luxuries.

HOW REALLY TO ENJOY THAT TRIP ABROAD

You'll find, just as so many other people have, that you really enjoy a trip abroad all year long when you haven't been trapped with "pay later" obligations. It is easy to avoid the "pay later" blues. Open a special vacation account at your mutual savings bank. Save regularly each payday and your savings bank will periodically add interest dividends. By the time you're ready to go abroad, you'll have the money you need to pay now and enjoy your trip now—and later, too.

Chapter Eleven

Buying a Car

SCENE: *Space Exploration Headquarters on Mars. Two Martians have just returned to their flying saucer after their first visit to Earth. They are reporting to their Superior.*

SUPERIOR: *"Well, how did you make out?"*

FIRST MARTIAN: *"We couldn't land, sir—it was too dangerous. We sampled the atmosphere and found a high content of noxious chemicals. So we circled around about 300 miles above the surface."*

SUPERIOR: *"Did you observe any signs of life below?"*

SECOND MARTIAN: *"Yes, we did. We used the long-range scope with the atmospheric penetration beam. There is definitely life on Earth."*

SUPERIOR: *"What sort of life?"*

FIRST MARTIAN: *"Several varieties, but the dominant form seems to be metallic. We could see millions of metal monsters moving around on wheels. Occasionally they would stop and little human slaves would feed them intravenously."*

119

Perhaps this bit of whimsy is not as fanciful as it seems. There are more than 60 million families in the United States, but they are heavily outnumbered by more than 100 million registered motor vehicles. As our clogged highways and polluted air will attest, the problems arising from our burgeoning automotive population are growing.

Before your family rushes off to the nearest showroom to invest several thousand dollars in a metal monster, some people may well say you will be doing both society and your pocketbook a favor by asking: is this trip really necessary?

Do you genuinely *need* a car?

Are you buying transportation you must have—or are you buying a status symbol?

Have you done your financial arithmetic on the cost of owning and operating a car? Here are a few things to keep in mind.

The cost of driving

Buying a car is an expensive proposition, much more expensive than it may seem at first glance. U.S. consumers spend about $45 billion each year for approximately 8 million new passenger cars and the same number of used cars.

The average cost of a new car can be expected to run well in excess of $3,000. But this is only the beginning. Here are estimates of other expenses you can expect to run up.

OPERATIONAL COSTS PER YEAR

Insurance	$160
Gasoline and oil	280
Maintenance	85
Tires	50
Tolls, parking, etc.	15
License and registration	24
	$614

These are conservative estimates and do not include the cost of garaging or the costs of financing if the car is bought on the installment plan. Nor are depreciation costs included here. But it is apparent that a $3,000 new car is going to cost at least another $3,000 to operate and maintain over a period of five years.

In addition, a car completely depreciates five years after you buy it and by that time will have practically no cash value. This means that it will depreciate, on the average, at an annual rate of $600. Add the annual $600-plus operational and maintenance costs to the annual depreciation rate of $600—and you get a minimum total cost of $1,200 per year to own a car.

If you finance the car through an installment loan, its actual cost to you will be higher still. If you can't pay cash for a new car, the most economical way to buy one on credit is through a savings bank passbook loan or an installment loan. This will keep your net financing cost to a minimum, as explained in a preceding chapter. Other sources, usually more expensive, for new-car loans are commercial banks, finance companies that have no connections with auto dealers, or dealers who will arrange the financing for you.

If you borrow directly from a small loan company, your financing costs will rise still further—anywhere from 33 to 45 percent in terms of true annual interest for a three-year loan of the cash you'll turn over to the dealer.

When you are financing a used-car purchase, you should expect the cost of your loan to be equally high, its term shorter, and the amount you can borrow to be smaller, since the risk to the lender will be greater than on a new-car loan. In New York, for example, a maximum true annual interest rate of 26 percent may be charged for used-car financing.

For the most part, we are a nation of brand-name buyers. We often develop strange loyalties to certain products, overlooking the fact that their intrinsic merits may vary from year to year. This is especially true in the field of automobiles. If you favor a Ford early in life, you may stick to this make later on. If you like Chevies, you may continue to buy Chevies more often than not. Plymouth people tend to remain Plymouth people. And so on.

But few industries have as much variation in the quality of their products from one year to the next as the automobile industry. If you want the most automobile for your money, forget about brand loyalties. Assume that all makes are fundamentally the same and begin to choose from there.

Choosing your model

If your family is of average size and has average transportation needs, how much sense does it make to buy a high-powered eight-cylinder car when a six-cylinder model will fill your needs adequately at a considerable saving in fuel costs?

The great mystery about American car buying is the popularity of the two-door hardtop. *Consumer Reports* comments: "It is ironic that the 2-door hardtop is the most widely sold body type since it costs more than a 4-door sedan, and it has more drawbacks and inconveniences in use than any body type except the convertible coupe. Most useful is the 4-door sedan; it is less given to rattles, squeaks and drafts, it offers more protection in an accident and it's easier to get into and out of."

A six-cylinder, four-door sedan may well be your best buy—if you can overcome those ego impulses and Junior's plea for a two-door convertible.

Don't ruin the economies already effected by splurging on a lot of unnecessary extras. Power windows will cost you $100 or so more—but do you really need them? What is the advantage of power brakes? They do make driving somewhat easier, but they won't stop the car more quickly, they cost more and they can be a problem on slippery highways or when driving at low speed.

Air conditioning is a convenience, but it will take a big bite out of your wallet. Prices run as high as $500 per unit, and there are both advantages and disadvantages to consider. If you live in a semitropical part of the country and will be using the equipment most of the year, you may have a real need for it. For someone living in the north, the need may be more imaginary than real. Granted that there are invariably some uncomfortable days in July and August, but will you get $500 worth of comfort out of air conditioning while driving on these days? On the plus side, even for people who live in a colder climate, is the fact that trade-in values for cars with air conditioning are higher than for those without it.

Used cars

The family has decided on the model, resolved to forgo all the superficial glitter and unnecessary extras and lined up its financing. You are now ready to decide:

A new car or a used car? Which make?

By all means buy a new car if you can afford it. Unless you are prepared to take it apart, you just won't know what you're getting if you buy a car somebody else (maybe several previous owners) has been driving. No matter how good the car turns out to be, your repair and fuel bills will be higher. So will your financing charges.

If you do opt for a used car, try to buy one from the new-car dealer first. He usually maintains a service shop, for one thing. For another, you will get first crack at the trade-ins, because he normally gets them first. Most used-car dealers get their inventory from auctions, and the cars that are auctioned off to them often are the poorer trade-ins that couldn't make the market after the new-car dealer had taken a look at them.

Above all, don't buy *any* used car without having it thoroughly checked out by an unbiased mechanic. Drive

123

the car yourself, testing the brakes and everything else you can think of. Also ask about guarantees and warranties. You'll be lucky if the dealer backs up his sale beyond 30 days. However, the used car you want may not have used up the original warranty or guarantee—it covers the car, not the owner.

Now for the question of make:

Here, too, you need an unbiased authority. A good source is *Consumer Reports*. Each year the January, February and March issues cover the 350 or so models and makes, and the April issue contains a special automotive roundup. The magazine will tell you—by year, model and make—which are the "Desirable Models" and the "Undesirable Models." You'll do well to be guided accordingly.

Automobile insurance

In almost every state of the U.S. a motorist must show that he is financially responsible—that he will be able to pay a specified amount for injury to a person or damage to property in any accident in which he may be involved, whether or not he caused the accident. He needs to show he can pay the money, in case he has to. This specified amount in some cases can go as high as $30,000 or more. Most people find that the best way to prove such financial responsibility is through automobile insurance.

In some states, in fact, auto insurance is mandatory. Bear in mind that the financial responsibility required by state law is not to cover *you*. It applies to the bodily injury and property damage for which you may become legally liable—the injury and damage suffered by someone else.

The most common form of minimum state-required responsibility is known as 10/20/5, although there are some variations among the states. A 10/20/5 requirement means that the motorist can pay $10,000 maximum to one person, $20,000 maximum for injuries to two or more people in the same accident, and $5,000 maximum for property damage an accident, often not enough protection.

In addition, you certainly should have some form of insurance that covers *you* and the members of your family, since there is the possibility that you might get hurt or wreck your car in an accident. Be sure that your auto insurance policy includes medical payments coverage. This would pay for any injuries that you or others riding in your car might suffer, no matter who was at fault in the accident.

Collision coverage

There is also collision insurance, which would reimburse you for damage to your own car—again, no matter who caused the damage. This form of insurance is usually sold with a deductible amount: you would pay the first $50 or $100 worth of damage and the insurance company would pay the rest.

Uninsured motorist coverage is also important. Under this arrangement, your own insurance company would pay you in the event you are injured by a driver of an uninsured car or by a hit-and-run driver, provided the accident was the other person's fault. In most cases it covers only injury to you or others in your car, although in a few states it also covers your car damage.

You also should carry what is called "comprehensive" insurance, which protects you in the event your car is damaged by fire, windstorm, flood, vandalism, theft and other perils.

You can include all these kinds of coverage in one car insurance policy.

Most companies offer a "special package" policy, which is about 10 percent less expensive than the regular policy because it eliminates duplicate payments of medical and hospital bills that may be covered by Blue Cross and Blue Shield or by some other form of health insurance.

The coverage of course is only up to the amount of the   125 policy. Don't drive without some form of insurance coverage beyond the minimum requirements. If you've lately checked the accident rate—*and medical costs*—you'll know why. Jury verdicts also are high, reaching in some cases up to a million dollars and are often within a range of $250,000 and $500,000, reflecting high medical costs.

The cost variables

The premium a driver pays for insurance depends on many factors: age, sex, marital status, use to which the car is put, size and value of car, area where the car is used, whether or not the driver (generally if he is under 25) has had high school driver education, the driver's record of accidents and serious traffic violations, the number of cars owned, the amount of protection you've bought, and so on. However, company rates do vary, so it is advisable to shop around.

HOW TO GET THE BEST DEAL ON THAT CAR

The compact auto you want costs about $2,000 plus .... Here's one way you can "borrow" that $2,000 ahead of time and earn dividends while you're "borrowing": start planning two years **before** you buy and open a "car account" in a mutual savings bank. "Borrow" $20 a week from your take-home income and pay it into this account. That averages out to better than $86 a month and it adds up to deposits of $1,040 a year—$2,080 in two years.

Add to this the money from the mutual savings interest dividend—it's money you have been earning while "borrowing"—and you are ready to go into the dealer's showroom with cash in hand. Nobody—absolutely nobody—will give you a better car-financing deal than that.

**A Workbook
To Help You
Record and Plan
Your Family's
Financial Affairs**

SOURCES OF ANNUAL FAMILY INCOME

Source	Last Year	This Year	Next Year (Estimate)
1. Take-home pay			
2. Payments from any profit-sharing plan			
3. Bonus			
4. Interest from all savings accounts			
5. Any tax refunds			
6. Gifts (Christmas, birthdays, other)			
7. Insurance policy dividends			
8. Stock dividends, bond interest			
9. Money from sale of car, house, etc.			
10. Profits from sale of any stocks, savings bonds			
11. Other income			
TOTAL			

BASIC ANNUAL FAMILY EXPENDITURES

Item	Last Year	This Year	Next Year (Estimate)
Housing			
Food			
Savings			
Medical expenses			
Clothing			
Transportation (car or other)			
Insurance premiums			
Taxes Income			
Property			
Other			
Home maintenance and improvement			
Education			
Vacation			
Entertainment			
Contributions			
Gifts			
Other items			
TOTAL			

PLAN YOUR SHORT-TERM SAVINGS GOALS

(less than one year)

Goal	Amount Needed	Dollars to Save Monthly	Date to Start	Date to Achieve
1. Vacation				
2. Christmas				
3.				
4.				
5.				

PLAN YOUR MEDIUM-TERM SAVINGS GOALS

(from one to three years)

Goal	Amount Needed	Dollars to Save Monthly	Date to Start	Date to Achieve
1. Baby				
2. Appliances				
3. Furnishings				
4. Car				
5. Boat				
6.				
7.				

PLAN YOUR LONG-TERM SAVINGS GOALS

(more than three years)

Goal 1	Amount Needed	Dollars to Save Monthly	Year to Start	Year to Achieve
House				
(Down Payment)				
Goal 2				
Children's				
College				
Education				
Goal 3				
Retirement				
Goal 4				
Other				

MONTHLY BUDGET WORKSHEETS

MONTHLY TAKE-HOME PAY

JANUARY

Expenses	Monthly Payments	Budget	Actual
1. Housing (principal, interest) Housing (rent)			
2. Food			
3. Savings			
4. Medical			
5. Clothing			
6. Transportation			
7. Life insurance Medical " Mortgage " Other "			
9. Vacation			
10. Entertainment			
11. Other			

MONTHLY BUDGET WORKSHEETS

MONTHLY TAKE-HOME PAY

FEBRUARY

Expenses	Monthly Payments	Budget	Actual
1. Housing (principal, interest) Housing (rent)			
2. Food			
3. Savings			
4. Medical			
5. Clothing			
6. Transportation			
7. Life insurance Medical " Mortgage " Other "			
9. Vacation			
10. Entertainment			
11. Other			

MONTHLY BUDGET WORKSHEETS

MONTHLY TAKE-HOME PAY

Expenses	Monthly Payments	MARCH Budget	MARCH Actual
1. Housing (principal, interest) Housing (rent)			
2. Food			
3. Savings			
4. Medical			
5. Clothing			
6. Transportation			
7. Life insurance Medical " Mortgage " Other "			
9. Vacation			
10. Entertainment			
11. Other			

MONTHLY BUDGET WORKSHEETS

MONTHLY TAKE-HOME PAY

Expenses	Monthly Payments	APRIL Budget	APRIL Actual
1. Housing (principal, interest) Housing (rent)			
2. Food			
3. Savings			
4. Medical			
5. Clothing			
6. Transportation			
7. Life insurance Medical " Mortgage " Other "			
9. Vacation			
10. Entertainment			
11. Other			

MONTHLY BUDGET WORKSHEETS

MONTHLY TAKE-HOME PAY   MAY

Expenses	Monthly Payments	Budget	Actual
1. Housing (principal, interest) Housing (rent)			
2. Food			
3. Savings			
4. Medical			
5. Clothing			
6. Transportation			
7. Life insurance Medical " Mortgage " Other "			
9. Vacation			
10. Entertainment			
11. Other			

MONTHLY BUDGET WORKSHEETS

MONTHLY TAKE-HOME PAY   JUNE

Expenses	Monthly Payments	Budget	Actual
1. Housing (principal, interest) Housing (rent)			
2. Food			
3. Savings			
4. Medical			
5. Clothing			
6. Transportation			
7. Life insurance Medical " Mortgage " Other "			
9. Vacation			
10. Entertainment			
11. Other			

MONTHLY BUDGET WORKSHEETS

MONTHLY TAKE-HOME PAY | JULY

Expenses	Monthly Payments	Budget	Actual
1. Housing (principal, interest) Housing (rent)			
2. Food			
3. Savings			
4. Medical			
5. Clothing			
6. Transportation			
7. Life insurance Medical " Mortgage " Other "			
9. Vacation			
10. Entertainment			
11. Other			

MONTHLY BUDGET WORKSHEETS

MONTHLY TAKE-HOME PAY | AUGUST

Expenses	Monthly Payments	Budget	Actual
1. Housing (principal, interest) Housing (rent)			
2. Food			
3. Savings			
4. Medical			
5. Clothing			
6. Transportation			
7. Life insurance Medical " Mortgage " Other "			
9. Vacation			
10. Entertainment			
11. Other			

MONTHLY BUDGET WORKSHEETS

MONTHLY TAKE-HOME PAY

SEPTEMBER

Expenses	Monthly Payments	Budget	Actual
1. Housing (principal, interest) Housing (rent)			
2. Food			
3. Savings			
4. Medical			
5. Clothing			
6. Transportation			
7. Life insurance Medical " Mortgage " Other "			
9. Vacation			
10. Entertainment			
11. Other			

MONTHLY TAKE-HOME PAY

OCTOBER

Expenses	Monthly Payments	Budget	Actual
1. Housing (principal, interest) Housing (rent)			
2. Food			
3. Savings			
4. Medical			
5. Clothing			
6. Transportation			
7. Life insurance Medical " Mortgage " Other "			
9. Vacation			
10. Entertainment			
11. Other			

MONTHLY BUDGET WORKSHEETS

MONTHLY TAKE-HOME PAY

NOVEMBER

Expenses	Monthly Payments	Budget	Actual
1. Housing (principal, interest) Housing (rent)			
2. Food			
3. Savings			
4. Medical			
5. Clothing			
6. Transportation			
7. Life insurance Medical " Mortgage " Other "			
9. Vacation			
10. Entertainment			
11. Other			

MONTHLY BUDGET WORKSHEETS

MONTHLY TAKE-HOME PAY

DECEMBER

Expenses	Monthly Payments	Budget	Actual
1. Housing (principal, interest) Housing (rent)			
2. Food			
3. Savings			
4. Medical			
5. Clothing			
6. Transportation			
7. Life insurance Medical " Mortgage " Other "			
9. Vacation			
10. Entertainment			
11. Other			

COLLEGE FUND PLAN   (First child)

Child's name	
Number of years to freshman college year	
Estimated amount needed for tuition and living costs	
Yearly:	
Total:	
Sources of college funds (total estimate)	
Savings	
Gifts	
Inheritance	
Trust fund	
Insurance policies	
Stocks and bonds	
Education loan	
Other	
TOTAL	

COLLEGE FUND PLAN   (Second child)

Child's name
Number of years to freshman college year
Estimated amount needed for tuition and living costs
Yearly:
Total:
Sources of college funds (total estimate)
Savings
Gifts
Inheritance
Trust fund
Insurance policies
Stocks and bonds
Education loan
Other
TOTAL

COLLEGE STUDENT'S FOUR-YEAR PLAN   (First child)

Income Source	Freshman	Sophomore	Junior	Senior
Allowance				
Earnings				
Savings fund				
Gifts				
Scholarships				
Education loan				
Trust fund				
Insurance policies				
Other				
TOTAL AVAILABLE FUNDS				

COLLEGE STUDENT'S FOUR-YEAR PLAN (Second child)

Income Source	Freshman	Sophomore	Junior	Senior
Allowance				
Earnings				
Savings fund				
Gifts				
Scholarships				
Education loan				
Trust fund				
Insurance policies				
Other				
TOTAL AVAILABLE FUNDS				

LOCATION OF IMPORTANT PAPERS
(include identification numbers, where appropriate)

Birth certificates	
Wills	
Savings passbooks	
Insurance policies	
Property deeds	
Stocks	
Bonds	
Other	

About the Author

Edward T. O'Toole has been writing about financial matters for the average citizen, and about economic affairs for the financial community, for more than 20 years. He knows finance intimately—he spent years in banking—and he has further studied it as a journalist. A staff member of *The New York Times* from 1961 to 1966, he covered every kind of savings and financial institution, including the stock market.

In 1963, the *Times* sent him to Europe. He opened the *Times* Brussels bureau and covered the European Common Market, the international money market and other European economic developments.

His previous book, "The New World of Banking," was published in 1965. He also has written many magazine articles on financial subjects on a free-lance basis and as managing editor of *Finance Magazine* and *Mergers and Acquisitions Magazine*.

A native New Yorker, he was educated at Brooklyn Prep, Fordham College and Syracuse University and is married to the former Susan Brennan. They live with their two children—and a coal black schnauzer named Spritzel —in Bronxville, New York.